S. Hrg. 114–740

CORRUPTION, VIOLENT EXTREMISM, KLEPTOCRACY, AND THE DANGERS OF FAILING GOVERNANCE

HEARING

BEFORE THE

COMMITTEE ON FOREIGN RELATIONS
UNITED STATES SENATE

ONE HUNDRED FOURTEENTH CONGRESS

SECOND SESSION

JUNE 30, 2016

Printed for the use of the Committee on Foreign Relations

Available via the World Wide Web:
http://www.govinfo.gov

U.S. GOVERNMENT PUBLISHING OFFICE

27–955 PDF   WASHINGTON : 2018

For sale by the Superintendent of Documents, U.S. Government Publishing Office
Internet: bookstore.gpo.gov   Phone: toll free (866) 512–1800; DC area (202) 512–1800
Fax: (202) 512–2104   Mail: Stop IDCC, Washington, DC 20402–0001

(II)

CONTENTS

CORRUPTION, VIOLENT EXTREMISM, KLEPTOCRACY, AND THE DANGERS OF FAILING GOVERNANCE

THURSDAY, JUNE 30, 2016

U.S. SENATE,
COMMITTEE ON FOREIGN RELATIONS,
Washington, DC.

The committee met, pursuant to notice, at 10:32 a.m. in Room SD–419, Dirksen Senate Office Building, Hon. Bob Corker, chairman of the committee, presiding.

Present: Senators Corker, Rubio, Perdue, Cardin, and Menendez.

OPENING STATEMENT OF HON. BOB CORKER, U.S. SENATOR FROM TENNESSEE

The CHAIRMAN. The Foreign Relations Committee will come to order.

We thank our outstanding witnesses for being with us today.

There will be probably fewer people here today. I think you all know voting ended yesterday and a lot of people headed out to do other things. But I do want to thank Senator Cardin and Senator Menendez for being here.

And I want to thank Senator Cardin for his continued push in regard to this particular topic, and certainly the two of you for the way you have championed making sure we do everything we can to rid our world of corruption.

We will consider the huge challenge of corruption and the extent to which widespread and pervasive public breach of trust internationally can undermine our most important national interests.

Our witness today will point out that corruption goes far beyond the loss of foreign aid dollars and foreign corrupt practices such as bribery and places our businesses at a competitive disadvantage.

Public corruption can undermine our most important interests in security and stability. Our witnesses today will argue there is a direct connection between the abuse of authority and the breakdown in governance.

In some cases, widespread abuses can stoke the fires of populism against corrupt governments, increasing the chances of instability or even violence. In the most extreme cases, we risk seeing important countries fall prey to predatory officials determined to enrich themselves at the cost of their citizens' welfare. Such states, when coupled a government monopoly on power, can present extraordinary national security risk to the United States.

If we want to fight corruption effectively and institute norms of government accountability, we have to develop smart strategies that allow us to target efforts at multiple levels of government and the population at large. We must be firm but fair, recognizing that cultivating a culture of public integrity may, in many countries, take a very, very long time. The challenge for us is to help governments make progress on reducing corruption while still continuing to work with them on a range of issues important to us.

And with that, I will turn it over to our distinguished ranking member and friend, Ben Cardin.

STATEMENT OF HON. BENJAMIN L. CARDIN, U.S. SENATOR FROM MARYLAND

Senator CARDIN. Well, Mr. Chairman, first of all, thank you for your extraordinary leadership of this committee to deal with good governance and corruption issues. We were together today at the State Department on the release of the 2016 Trafficking in Persons Report. There is no stronger advocate for a strong U.S. position on stopping modern day slavery than our chairman, Senator Corker. And we thank you.

And as I will point out during this hearing, trafficking in persons is horrible, 20 million victims. But it is fueled by corruption, people making a lot of corrupt money off of trafficking in persons. So it is very much related to the hearing we have today.

And I have really looked forward to this hearing for many reasons. Two of those reasons are that our first witnesses on the panel, Gayle Smith, our Administrator of the USAID, does an incredible job and has had a critical career, and Tom Malinowski, the Assistant Secretary for Democracy, Human Rights, and Labor, our inside person at the State Department on these issues—we appreciate very much both of your leadership on dealing with corruption.

There is a growing recognition in the United States and around the world of the threat that corruption presents to international security and stability. We have all seen the headlines about corruption and feel like it is pervasive from scandals in places such as Brazil and Malaysia to doping of Russian athletes and their subsequent ban from the Summer Olympics, to the Panama Papers. What is certainly becoming clear is that where there is a high level of corruption, we find fragile states are states suffering from internal or external conflicts, places such as Afghanistan and Pakistan, Iraq, Syria, Somalia, Nigeria, and Sudan. Corruption and the dysfunction that follows it fuels violent extremism. Corruption becomes a deeply held grievance that mutates into a basis for revolutions that spin out of control.

Just 2 weeks ago, we heard in this committee how corruption feeds the fire of criminal networks and transnational crime. Corruption pushes young people towards violence and extremism because they lose faith in the institutions that are supposed to protect and serve them. They lose faith in the compact between government and the people, and terrorist groups use corruption to recruit followers in their hateful crimes.

The human cost of corruption is substantial. Here are just two examples.

First, this morning, the State Department released its annual TIP Report, as I pointed out. Corruption is a constant companion to modern day slavery and the suffering that it brings. We have also seen this in the refugees and migrant crisis where thousands have lost their lives in the Mediterranean, victims of trafficking networks and corrupt government officials who facilitate illicit business.

And make no mistake about it. Corruption is a very big business. One news report estimates that traffickers made between $5 billion to $6 billion in 2015 alone in brining approximately 1 million refugees and migrants to Europe.

Corruption also damages our foreign assistance efforts. This is U.S. taxpayer dollars that we are using that we have a responsibility to make sure is used most effectively. Our development efforts are undermined when people decide that siphoning off money makes more sense than using it for its intended purpose. In our work training security forces and police, corruption drains the will of good people to serve their country, robs forces of necessary equipment, and undermines the very effort to build capable institutions that can protect and serve.

It is also costing us. According to one estimate, between 2003 and 2012, the international community has lost $6.6 trillion to illicit outflows of money that was intended to do good, not harm.

As I indicated several times, it just operates just opposite of what we are trying to do. So if we are using our taxpayer dollars and that is fueling corruption, that is accomplishing the exact opposite purpose for why we have development assistance and security assistance.

We need a larger sum of our efforts to be put into good governance and to deal with these issues so that we can effectively deal with the other missions which development assistance and security assistance is aimed to do.

I want to make it clear that the United States has been doing a lot of good work on anti-corruption. The Department for Democracy, Human Rights, and Labor has focused on governance programs to build civil society capacity, which I believe is essential and using open government partnership as a tool to monitor commitments by countries to fight corruption. USAID is implementing programs to embed a culture of accountability and international standards to limit the opportunities for corruption to thrive.

But the problem of corruption is growing, not shrinking. We must meet the scale of the problem with greater resolve and commitment. To do that, I believe we should focus on four things, and let me just mention them very quickly, Mr. Chairman.

First, we must institutionalize the fight against corruption as a national security priority. Yes, corruption is part of the State Department's annual human rights report, but it is just a small portion of it. Ensuring that bureaus and our missions overseas prioritize corruption in their struggle, planning is essential.

Second, we need a whole government effort, and let us be better coordinated. Right now, we work across multiple agencies and multiple offices on corruption. There is much information on best practices that needs to be shared.

Third, we need to find ways to fund anti-corruption work. We need resources. Corruption is a big business and big money. We should look at ways that we can use seized assets or ill-gotten proceeds to build civil society capacity to fight corruption and make it easier to transfer these assets to the appropriate effort.

And fourth, we must improve our oversight of foreign and security assistance and promote transparency. Yesterday, the Senate passed the Foreign Assistance Transparency and Accountability Act, which was sponsored by Senator Rubio and myself. Mr. Chairman, thank you for your help not only in getting it out of the committee, but getting it through the process. This bill will shine a light on foreign aid and ensure that U.S. foreign assistance programs are measured adequately and appropriately. It also empowers civil societies in recipient countries to combat corruption.

And secondly, through the Cardin-Lugar provisions of the Dodd-Frank Act, section 1504, I have pushed for greater revenue transparency in extractive sectors because we know that secrecy breeds corruption. After 6 long years, the SEC finally has issued its regulation, and it is a strong regulation. After we acted 6 years ago, a lot of other countries have passed what we consider to be the right standard for extractive industries to show where their contracts are so you can trace the money. We now regain our leadership through this regulation on transparency.

We want, as you know, the resources of a nation not to be a curse but to help bring them out of poverty. We want our development assistance to be a help to a country and not fuel corruption.

These are two great successes, the transparency bill and the SEC regulations, and we hope that we can build on that.

So let me be clear-eyed. The fight against corruption is long and difficult, and I know that we have to stay committed to this end. I am very much encouraged by the efforts I see of my colleagues.

And I do look forward to hearing from our witnesses.

The CHAIRMAN. Thank you. Thank you very much for those comments.

We have two panels today, and our first witness today is the Honorable Gayle Smith, Administrator for the U.S. Agency for International Development. I am glad she has assumed this role and believe that her preexisting relationship with the White House is something that greatly benefits USAID. And we are looking forward to your testimony.

Our second witness on the panel today is the Honorable Tom Malinowski, Assistant Secretary for the Bureau of Democracy, Human Rights, and Labor at the State Department. I first met Tom over an adult beverage in Munich when he was on the outside, and I look forward to having one when he is finished with this job to tell me the differences between being on the outside and on the inside. [Laughter.]

The CHAIRMAN. But today, we look forward to his testimony.

And with that, if you could summarize your comments in about 5 minutes or so, and without objection, your written comments will be entered into the record. But if you would begin, Gayle, we would appreciate it. Again, thank you for being here.

STATEMENT OF HON. GAYLE SMITH, ADMINISTRATOR, U.S. AGENCY FOR INTERNATIONAL DEVELOPMENT, WASHINGTON, D.C.

Ms. SMITH. Thank you and I will be brief.

Thank you, Chairman Corker and Senator Cardin and members of the committee, for the opportunity to discuss USAID's work to combat corruption across the globe.

I also want to thank you for your continued leadership and ongoing commitment to elevate this issue and advance accountability and transparency, and I would fully concur that it has been a very good week.

As you know, corruption tears at the fabric of society and hinders inclusive economic growth and democratic governance. It also poses major security risks to the United States, often enabling radicalization and fueling political instability and conflict.

At AID, we measure the effects of corruption in dollars lost, missed opportunities for inclusive economic growth and development, the erosion of public confidence in government, and rising insecurity.

As risks and threats posed by corruption continue to increase, however, we are also seeing some small but important new windows of opportunity emerge, including an increased citizens' demand for accountability and transparency, the growing commitment of some political leaders, and an emerging global consensus embodied in many places but also in the sustainable development goals that effective governance and strong institutions are required to sustain development outcomes.

Building on decades of U.S. leadership, President Obama has made fighting corruption a national security priority. With a diverse array of agencies engaged in anti-corruption work, each with comparative advantage and different missions, authorities, and tools, the United States is able to attack corruption from every angle, including through building and enforcing the rule of law, enhancing the disclosure, detection, and prevention of corrupt practices, developing capacity in institutions, and engaging civil society, foreign governments, and multilateral institutions as partners.

For USAID, global anti-corruption efforts also include the promotion of human rights, participatory democracy, transparent governance, the role for a vibrant civil society, and economic empowerment.

As the United States' lead development agency with programs in more than 100 countries worldwide, USAID's primary role within the U.S. strategy is to empower citizens, embed norms and standards, and build accountable and transparent institutions. Where we can enlist governments and their citizens as able and willing partners, we are increasing the scale and impact of anti-corruption efforts in the countries, regions, and sectors in which we operate. We do this in four ways: first, advancing accountability; second, improving open, effective, and democratic governance; third, strengthening adherence to international norms and standards; and fourth, leading multilateral efforts to tackle corruption.

From a development perspective, accountability is most effectively sustained when a vibrant civil society has the rights, capacity, and tools to hold governments, businesses, and citizens to account. Through our support for civil society, USAID and our partners enhance the capacity of citizen watchdogs to oversee local public spending, promote community development, reconstruction, and monitor the delivery of services.

A recent example where USAID and the State Department are supporting civil society is in the case of support for investigative journalists, including for the organized crime and corruption reporting project which has recently helped expose the scope and nature of corruption around the world.

As we support citizens who are demanding change and help build their capacity to hold their governments accountable, we must also support governments as they work to strengthen their institutions and develop more effective and efficient systems with built-in transparency.

For example, we helped Honduras establish the country's first legal assistance and anti-corruption complaint center, and our support for tax and custom reform in Georgia helped decrease business expectations of corruption by tax officials by more than 80 percent.

USAID also has an important role to play in developing and embedding the international norms and standards that incentivize anti-corruption actions. Through the Extractive Industries Transparency initiative, USAID has helped strengthen a powerful and visible platform to increase revenue transparency and accountability in the natural resources sector.

USAID also helps emerging democracies meet their obligations under a number of international standards for transparency, including the U.N. Convention Against Corruption, EITI, and the SDGs.

Additionally, USAID forges partnerships with other donors, multilateral agencies, and civil society organizations to help leverage and sustain local initiatives and to help enable the sharing of best practices and replication. The 70-country strong Open Government Partnership has been effective in engaging the interest of governments in greater transparency and a role for civil society to hold them accountable. And USAID supports efforts to help countries become eligible and assists member countries with their national action plans.

The last thing I want to touch on is how we are working to safeguard USAID's own investments. We continually look for new opportunities to improve our monitoring approaches and have developed tools like the Public Financial Management Risk Assessment Framework to assess the capabilities of partner governments and other recipients to properly administer funds. Even with the smart steps we have taken and careful measures we put in place, we remain vigilant because of access constraints and other difficulties in the places we work.

We are committed to working closely with Congress to prevent corruption and other misuses of taxpayer dollars and equally committed to taking swift action upon learning of any such abuse.

Thank you again for this opportunity. We share with you your diagnosis and analysis of the problem and hope we can work together to expand on the areas where we are having success and redouble our efforts in those areas that need more attention. Thank you.

[Ms. Smith's prepared statement follows:]

PREPARED STATEMENT OF GAYLE E. SMITH

Chairman Corker, Ranking Member Cardin, and distinguished members of the Committee: thank you for inviting me here to discuss the United States Agency for International Development's work to combat corruption across the globe. I want to thank you for shining a light on this important topic, and for your continued leadership and ongoing commitment to root out corruption and advance accountability and transparency.

Corruption takes on many forms, from the bribery of public officials to collusion in public procurement to the wholesale theft of government assets. Although its different forms may cause varying degrees of harm, corruption as a whole tears at the fabric of society and hinders inclusive economic growth and democratic governance. Additionally, corruption poses major security risks to the United States, often enabling radicalization and violent extremism and fueling political instability and conflict. That is why President Obama views corruption as a fundamental obstacle to peace, prosperity, and human rights, and our Administration has sought to elevate anti-corruption efforts across our foreign policy and development agendas.

As the United States' lead development agency, USAID plays a critical role in the U.S. Government's strategy to stem the tide of corruption and hold to account all those who exploit the public trust for private gain. Our work takes us to every corner of the world, where we have seen firsthand the devastating impacts corruption can have on people, communities, and countries. But, encouragingly, we are also seeing new and promising trends on which to build.

Bolstered by the strong model of transparency and accountability the United States has constructed here at home, the fight against corruption has become increasingly central to our international development policy and strategy. As we continue to work with our partners to foster sustained and inclusive economic growth and promote open, effective, and democratic governance around the world, we are integrating anti-corruption efforts into the way the Agency does business—across borders and across sectors.

THE MANY COSTS OF CORRUPTION

For the countries where USAID works, the costs of corruption are significant and lasting. In some severe cases of systemic corruption, we have seen substantial portions of country budgets lost to waste, fraud, and abuse, stalling and in some cases halting development progress altogether. In total, according to the United Nations, corruption, bribery, theft, and tax evasion cost developing countries approximately $1.26 trillion each year.

But the losses caused by corruption are not measured in dollars alone. We can also see the effects of corruption in missed opportunities for economic growth and development. Corruption lowers the confidence of the private sector in developing economies, hampering prospects for investment that can catalyze growth. Corruption siphons away scarce resources from public investments in much-needed social services and the productive sectors which fuel economic growth. It is worth noting that these opportunity costs are felt most acutely by the world's poor, who depend on those services and stand to benefit the most from economic empowerment. Women, too, disproportionately suffer the impacts of corruption.

The costs of corruption are also evident in the eroding public confidence in government. Poor governance and corruption alienates publics in democracies and entrenched authoritarian regimes alike, as they see that a few people benefit from their connections while larger numbers of people are left out.

Additionally, systemic corruption fuels rising insecurity and enables dangerous transnational threats. The more corrupt an environment is, the easier it is for violent extremists to establish themselves as an alternative to ruling elites perceived to be immoral and unaccountable. Endemic corruption can also provide extremist groups with the enabling environment they need to access financial systems and align with criminal and other illicit networks.

EMERGING OPPORTUNITIES TO TACKLE CORRUPTION

Even as risks and threats posed by corruption continue to increase, we are seeing new windows of opportunity emerge. First, all across the world, there is growing popular demand for increased accountability and transparency from governments. It was a call to end corruption that helped spur the Tunisian revolution in 2010, and that same call drove hundreds of thousands of Ukrainians to the Maidan three years later. More recently the release of the Panama Papers turned the world's attention to illicit financial activity by the wealthy and well-connected on every continent, spurring massive protests and the Prime Minister's resignation in Iceland and sparking outrage and debate from North America to Asia.

In Guatemala last year, where impunity once reigned, people took to the streets and spurred the legal and orderly removal of the sitting President and Vice President. All over the world, civil society has intensified its demands for honest government and seeks to remove corrupt leaders from office through elections, impeachment, prosecutions, or civil protest. Second, we are seeing more—though still insufficient—top-down interest in reform, as leaders are increasingly demonstrating a willingness to put political capital in the fight against corruption. Some governments have shown they have the political will to build the institutions required to reduce and prevent corruption, increase transparency of public revenues and finances, and enhance accountability for budgeting and delivery of services. For example, Senegal passed a sweeping transparency law in 2012, and the Tunisian Minister of Finance is working directly with USAID to root out corruption in tax and customs collections. The leaders of Nigeria and Afghanistan—two countries historically plagued by severe corruption—have each made significant commitments to combat corruption and have followed up with concrete actions. In Nigeria, where corruption in the oil sector is especially pervasive, President Buhari's administration has undertaken a series of reforms aimed at reducing graft and improving transparency, including a restructuring of the state-owned Nigerian National Petroleum Corporation.

And in Afghanistan, President Ghani is personally invested in the fight against corruption. Along with Chief Executive Officer Abdullah and senior ministers, he established and chairs the National Procurement Commission, which meets weekly. His government has created a new High Council on Good Governance, Corruption, and Justice to coordinate anti-corruption efforts throughout the government and is also working to implement recommendations made by the Afghanistan Independent Joint Anti-Corruption Monitoring and Evaluation Committee (MEC). At the invitation of the Afghan Ministry of Public Health, the MEC recently completed a comprehensive anticorruption assessment, and the recommendations of that public report are under review for implementation. Other ministries have volunteered for similar corruption assessments.

In recent months, I have met with the leaders of Ukraine, Albania, Georgia, and Guatemala. In each of these meetings, these leaders raised corruption as a major concern, and asked for support in dealing with specific aspects of the challenge, ranging from technical assistance on customs reform to experts on transparent financial management. This kind of engagement is a necessary first step on the long road to ending corruption.

Finally, a global consensus is now emerging that transparency and accountability are pre-requisites for achieving sustained and inclusive development progress. It was not long ago that the United States was one of few governments consistently championing transparency and accountability, but that is no longer the case. This new global consensus is embodied in the Sustainable Development Goals (SDGs), which world leaders from 193 countries endorsed in September 2015. In part due to the hard work and engagement of the U.S. Government, the goals explicitly recognize—through Goal 16—that corruption and related challenges hinder growth and progress. Importantly, the SDGs are more than just aspirational; they include targets against which governments—and their citizens—can measure progress. And growing multilateral partnerships like the Open Government Partnership are helping countries meet Goal 16 targets and pursue other governance reforms.

This global recognition has already translated into concrete commitments. In the Common African Position on the Post-2015 Development Agenda, African leaders affirmed their support for anticorruption efforts and committed to adopting new measures to fight corruption and strengthen good governance. As another example of the global consensus at work, in May 2016 leaders of more than 40 governments gathered in London to commit to deepen and widen the fight against corruption through better coordination of government action, including efforts to advance beneficial ownership transparency, to increase revenue transparency in key sectors including energy, and to share knowhow and data required to enforce laws against corruption and money laundering and to recover stolen assets

There is no question that the development, democratic governance, and security challenges posed by corruption have become more urgent and complex. But with increased citizen demand, growing commitment from leaders, and a shared global agenda, there is new and significant momentum behind U.S. efforts to attack corruption from all angles.

That is why—building on decades of U.S. leadership—President Obama has made fighting corruption a national security priority. The United States has been a leader in anti-corruption efforts since the Foreign Corrupt Practices Act (FCPA)—the first ever law prohibiting bribery of foreign officials—was enacted in 1977. Since then, U.S. Government agencies have developed a comprehensive, whole-of-government approach both to enforce the FCPA and other laws prohibiting corruption and to initiate policies and programs to institute good governance across the globe. In addition to USAID, those agencies include the Department of State, the Department of Justice, the Securities and Exchange Commission, the Department of the Treasury, the Department of Commerce, the Millennium Challenge Corporation, the Overseas Private Investment Corporation, the Trade and Development Agency, the United States Trade Representative, and others.

Each agency makes up a vital component of a comprehensive agenda that has helped make the United States the global standard-bearer in countering corruption both at home and across the globe. For example, the Treasury Department works to protect the U.S. financial system from abuse by illicit actors, including corrupt individuals. And the Department of Justice (DOJ) pursues corrupt foreign officials who plunder state coffers for personal gain and then try to place those funds within the U.S. financial system, while DOJ, the SEC, and their law enforcement partners pursue bribe paying individuals and companies over which the United States has jurisdiction.

The Overseas Private Investment Corporation and Trade and Development Agency seek to provide financial and technical support to countries that have consistently demonstrated progress in strengthening good governance. The Millennium Challenge Corporation incentivizes countries to demonstrate a positive track record and concrete plan to reduce corruption in order to achieve eligibility. The Department of Commerce, through commercial diplomacy and other initiatives abroad and in numerous international fora, promotes transparency and anti-corruption efforts in our trading partners in order to create a level playing field for U.S. businesses.

By engaging such a diverse array of agencies in anti-corruption work—each with different missions, authorities, and tools—the United States is able to attack corruption from every angle, including through building and enforcing the rule of law; enhancing the disclosure, detection, and prevention of corrupt practices; and engaging civil society, foreign governments, and multilateral institutions as partners. For USAID, U.S. global anti-corruption efforts also include the promotion of human rights, participatory democracy, accountable and transparent governance, and economic empowerment.

HOW USAID TACKLES CORRUPTION

USAID's primary role within the U.S. strategy is to empower citizens, embed norms and standards, and build accountable and transparent institutions. With programs in more than 100 countries worldwide, we are uniquely positioned on the front lines of the fight against global corruption. By leveraging this position—as well as our existing relationships with governments and civil society—we work to address corruption at its roots. And, where we can enlist governments and their citizens as able and willing partners, we are increasing the scale and impact of anti-corruption efforts in the countries, regions, and sectors in which we operate.

This is essential. Unless people, communities, and countries take ownership of their challenges and their progress, development cannot be sustainable or inclusive. The same is true for efforts to combat corruption. Guided by this principle, USAID works to be a strategic and effective partner of civil society and governments. We do this by: (1) advancing accountability, (2) improving open, effective, and democratic governance, (3) strengthening adherence to international norms and standards, and (4) promoting multilateral efforts to tackle corruption.

Advancing accountability

The United States should hold governments, corporations, organizations, and individuals to account through enforcement measures and by other means. But from a development perspective, accountability is most effectively sustained when a vibrant civil society has the rights, capacity, and tools to hold governments, businesses, and citizens to account. Through our support for civil society, USAID and our partners enhance the capacity of citizen watchdogs to oversee local public spending, promote community development and reconstruction, and monitor the delivery of services. The civil society groups we support also educate the public on their rights, and on the many different tools available to them.

For example, in Pakistan, USAID's Citizens' Voice Project (CVP) is supporting provincial governments to inform people about the Right to Information Act, a new law that grants citizens access to information previously withheld from the public. CVP has supported nearly 200 civil society groups to amplify citizen voices and facilitate productive engagement with the government. And in Paraguay, web-based programs developed to improve citizen oversight of government data helped unearth multiple cases of corruption. This exposure led to the firing of 1,000 ghost employees in the Ministry of Education who had been receiving salaries without actually working, and placed two members of Congress and the Chancellor of the National University under criminal investigation.

But the continuing backlash against civil society and closing of political space in countries across the globe compromises the ability of citizen groups to demand transparency and accountability. That's why we have joined our partners in the U.S. Government, governments around the world, the philanthropic community, and multilateral partners to push back against these emerging restrictions and dangerous trends. Through the President's Stand With Civil Society agenda, we work to improve the policy environment for civil society organizations, increase multilateral and diplomatic pressure against restrictive laws, and develop innovative ways to support civil society where it is under duress.

In some contexts, advancing accountability requires us to first help expose the nature and scope of corruption. This has the dual benefit of raising awareness among citizens and drawing the attention of prosecutorial and investigative bodies. One way we do this is through training investigative journalists and supporting high profile and high-impact reporting on corruption. In Fiscal Year 2015, USAID contributed approximately $30 million to support media development in more than 25 countries. This relatively small amount of funding can eventually pay significant dividends in terms of transparency, asset recovery, and other law enforcement actions.

For example, USAID, along with the State Department, supported the Organized Crime and Corruption Reporting Project (OCCRP), a network of investigative journalists working across Europe and Eurasia. OCCRP's reporting has resulted in the recovery of at least $600 million in hidden assets by tax authorities, as well as more than $2.8 billion in fines, seizures, and asset freezes. Additionally, 1,300 companies were closed and 80 people arrested because of illegal activity exposed by the group.

USAID also works to enhance accountability by improving the auditing capacity within governments. In April 2016, we signed a Memorandum of Understanding with the Government Accountability Office's Center for Audit Excellence to collaborate on training and technical assistance efforts to strengthen auditing organizations in developing countries.

Going forward, USAID will continue to support citizens as they expose corruption and hold their leaders accountable.

Improving open, effective, and democratic governance

Fighting corruption is also central to our core strategic goal of supporting democracy, human rights, and governance. As we support citizens who are demanding change, and help build their capacity to hold their governments accountable, we must also support governments as they work to strengthen their institutions and develop more efficient and effective systems—with built-in transparency. Our work to strengthen justice sectors offers a great example of this work. USAID is a global leader in the promotion of the rule of law, with a long history of joining with our interagency partners in supporting justice system reforms in every region of the world. This support includes a whole of government approach in developing training and professional development opportunities for judges and prosecutors, empowering them to take on corrupt officials and elites.

New technologies and innovations are accelerating our efforts. For example, we are installing computer automation to track cases in all 74 of Jordan's courts to improve judicial efficiency, and in Honduras we supported the establishment of the country's first Legal Assistance and Anti-Corruption Complaint Center. In Fiscal Year 2015, the Center tracked 65 formal corruption complaints, ultimately leading to 12 investigations.

Innovations and modernized systems are changing the way governments operate in other sectors as well. In vulnerable environments, we are leveraging programming in sectors like health and education to combat corruption. In countries with high vulnerability to corruption, we apply these innovative management systems in specific sectors like health and education, both to counter corruption and improve the delivery of services. To help governments collect revenues and budget more cost-effectively, we have helped implement standards of transparency and accountability for public financial management. And to help governments save costs, we have made great strides helping reform public procurement systems and institutionalize e-governance. These systems reduce opportunity for corrupt activity by limiting face-to-face interactions with public officials and automatically tracking all transactions.

For example, in Albania, we are supporting efforts to develop One-Stop Service Centers for all municipal transactions. These centers will help local governments be more responsive, while limiting room for corrupt practices. In some places, we are quickly seeing a sizable impact from these new systems. Less than five months after Ukraine introduced new electronic procurement software to cut down on opportunities for corruption, an estimated $65 million has already been saved.

In 2002, Georgia had one of the worst reputations in the former Soviet Union for bribe-taking and corruption, with more than 4 out of 5 businesses reporting that they were expected to give gifts in meetings with tax officials. After the Rose Revolution and subsequent 2004 elections, USAID partnered with the new government in support of a major reorganization and other reforms of the tax and customs departments. By 2008, only 8.4 percent of businesses continued to complain about expectations of corruption by tax officials—an astounding drop of more than 80 percent. And from 2002 to 2011, Georgia increased tax revenue by about 12.6 percent of GDP.

Not only do improved systems save money and increase revenue, they also offer an opportunity for governments to reinvest those savings in the growth of their economies and in the well-being of their people. This can occur in any sector. After USAID supported an analysis of the central and individual hospital payroll systems in the Dominican Republic, the Ministry of Public Health took action to clean the payroll. In total, the Ministry eliminated more than 4,000 ghost workers, leading to a savings of $9.5 million. And now, those savings are being used to hire health care workers and increase access to primary care across the country. The investments, along with the elimination of user fees and increased membership in national health insurance, are already paying off. One impoverished region witnessed a 500 percent increase in patient consultations over a one-year period.

As these kinds of successes continue to occur, more countries are likely to replicate the results, which will be necessary to achieve the scale we need. USAID will continue to build the evidence base for smart governance reforms across all of the sectors in which we work, just as we will continue to encourage the adoption of innovative systems and technologies.

Strengthening adherence to international norms and standards

USAID also has an important role to play in developing and embedding the international norms and standards that incentivize anti-corruption action. U.S. leadership has been essential in establishing and implementing the international legal frameworks that guide corruption enforcement today, such as the UN Convention Against Corruption (UNCAC) and the Organization for Economic Cooperation and Development Anti-Bribery Convention.

USAID has helped to establish a powerful and visible platform to strengthen international norms in the natural resources sector, a sector ripe for corrupt activity in many countries. The Extractive Industries Transparency Initiative (EITI) is a multi-stakeholder initiative to increase revenue transparency and create a new standard of accountability. With strong support from Congress, USAID has contributed more than $26 million between Fiscal Year 2008 and Fiscal Year 2015 to support country-led efforts to join or implement EITI.

By lifting up governments that are publishing key financial information or audit results, we showcase how these actions foster growth and make countries more attractive to foreign investment. In Peru, for example, we helped bring together oil and mining companies, government officials, and prominent civil society organizations to foster a dialogue on the benefits of EITI membership. And in 2012, Peru became the first country in Latin America to become EITI compliant.

USAID has helped emerging democracies meet their obligations under a number of other international standards for transparency and accountability, including UNCAC. Additionally, it is important that jurisdictions effectively implement the Financial Action Task Force global standards on anti-money laundering and countering the financing of terrorism, which include standards for the disclosure of true beneficial ownership of companies. Moving forward, every USAID mission will outline plans to support country-level SDG implementation in its five-year strategy, which includes support for meeting good governance and anti-corruption targets like the significant reduction of illicit finance by 2030.

We will continue to promote the adoption and adherence to the international norms and standards that provide a guide for global cooperation on combating corruption.

Promoting multilateral efforts to tackle corruption

Similarly, we will continue to bring the global community together in the fight against corruption. In many of the countries where we work, multilateral support and engagement is essential to help build the capacity and incentivize the steps required to achieve scale in our anti-corruption work. USAID forges partnerships with other donors, multilateral agencies, and civil society organizations to help leverage and sustain local initiatives and to help enable the sharing of best practices and replication.

The Open Government Partnership (OGP)—a multilateral initiative launched by the United States and seven other governments in 2011—is the most prominent example of this approach. With 70 countries now participating, OGP helps reform-minded officials and citizens promote transparency, engage, and harness new technologies to fight corruption and improve governance.

As a multilateral public platform, OGP has been effective in engaging the interest of governments in greater transparency, but that alone is not enough. That is why USAID supports efforts to help countries become eligible for the OGP, and assists member countries with the implementation of their National Action Plans. Once again, our efforts here are bolstered by U.S. leadership at home. The United States is also meeting its obligations under the OGP, including by submitting our own National Action Plan for civil society scrutiny. In addition to being good practice, this kind of leadership by example also gives us more credibility on the international stage. More than a dozen USAID missions plan to provide $14 million to support OGP in Fiscal Year 2015 and $10 million in Fiscal Year 2016.

OGP is a dynamic example of the preventive, positive and scalable USAID approach. Since its launch in 2011, it has grown quickly to include 70 countries and more than 2,000 commitments to undertake reforms jointly developed by government and citizens. Brazil, Croatia, and Sierra Leone all passed Access to Information Laws—some of which were stalled for years—in order to join the Partnership. Following the UK Anti-Corruption Summit in May, Nigeria became the latest country to join OGP and commit to fighting corruption at every level.

We have also supported multilateral engagement at the regional level. This approach has shown promise in strengthening the capabilities of internal government watchdogs, like inspectors general and other auditors. For example, the U.S.-Africa Partnership on Illicit Finance is designed to promote action to combat illicit finance in Africa. Senegal has joined the United States in developing a national action plan, and six other nations are writing their own.

And in the Middle East and North Africa, which has the least transparent and open budget process in the world according to the 2015 Open Budget Survey, we are supporting several countries—including Algeria, Egypt, Iraq, Morocco, and Tunisia—to implement international standards and best practices for government audit and oversight. And through the Effective Institutions Platform, we are helping support a learning alliance of Latin American Supreme Audit Institutions, and highlighting ways these institutions can strengthen their work to target government corruption and financial mismanagement.

PROTECTING TAXPAYER RESOURCES FROM CORRUPTION

The last thing I want to touch on is how we are working to safeguard USAID investments from corruption. This is absolutely essential.

We continually look for new opportunities to improve our monitoring approach and attack the challenges from every angle. For example, in Afghanistan, one of the most difficult places we work, USAID developed a multi-tiered monitoring approach. The approach allows project managers to gather and analyze data from multiple sources, triangulate information to increase our confidence in the reporting, and use the results to make programmatic decisions. In Syria, innovative tracking mechanisms are used to ensure targeted beneficiaries receive assistance; these include biometrics such as ID cards, fingerprints, or iris scans; electronic distribution of transfers; distinct marking of paper vouchers; regular in-person and unannounced visits to beneficiary households, distribution sites, or vendor shops. And in some places plagued by corruption, terrorism, violent extremism, and conflict—where our investments face the greatest risks—we conduct vetting programs to keep American funds out of the hands of bad actors.

We have also developed new tools to assess the capabilities of partner governments and other recipients to properly administer funds. One such tool is the Public Financial Management Risk Assessment Framework, which has led to several decisions not to utilize host government systems because of insufficient controls. Other practices like fixed obligation grants can ensure that disbursements are only made against agreed-upon results. Additionally, since 2012 Congress has required the publication of annual reports on fiscal transparency of governments that receive aid from the United States, ensuring that U.S. taxpayer money is used appropriately. These reviews also serve to sustain a dialogue with governments focused on improving their fiscal performance.

Of course, USAID's Inspector General is also essential to protecting taxpayer dollars and preventing fraud, waste, and abuse, and I want to thank the Committee for confirming Ann Calveresi-Barr to serve in this important role. USAID missions around the world greatly appreciate oversight from the Office of the Inspector General, often proactively requesting investigations.

The hard truth is that, even with the smart steps we have taken and careful measures we have put in place, we are sometimes vulnerable. USAID is called to serve in some of the most difficult environments imaginable, where access constraints often hinder our ability to ensure proper oversight of projects. Despite these constraints, we are committed to working closely with Congress to prevent corruption and other misuses of taxpayer dollars. And we are equally committed to taking swift action upon learning of any such abuse.

CONCLUSION

I want to thank you again for the opportunity to share with you the important work USAID is doing, as part of a larger U.S. whole-of-government strategy, to invest in the prevention and elimination of corruption worldwide. Our experience demonstrates that the most effective pathway to reaching scale is to help create compacts between citizens and governments that enable countries to institutionalize good governance, deliver social services efficiently and fairly and provide wide access to economic opportunity. Our leaders, staff and implementing partners will continue to prioritize and practice anti-corruption no matter which sector they work in.

Going forward, we will continue to make progress in infusing anti-corruption work into the bloodstream of the Agency, including through mission-led country strategies, our broader democracy and governance work, and through our sector-based programming in fields like global health and education. Further integration into the way we do business will be instrumental to implementing a comprehensive and successful long-term anti-corruption strategy. USAID shares this Committee's deep commitment to the values of transparency and accountability, and we will continue to promote them through our work to advance human rights and dignity around the world.

Thank you.

The CHAIRMAN. Thank you.

Mr. Malinowski.

STATEMENT OF HON. TOMASZ P. MALINOWSKI, ASSISTANT SECRETARY, BUREAU OF DEMOCRACY, HUMAN RIGHTS, AND LABOR, U.S. DEPARTMENT OF STATE, WASHINGTON, D.C.

Mr. MALINOWSKI. Thank you, Chairman Corker, Senator Cardin. Thank you for holding the hearing and for bringing increased attention to this challenge.

Let me start with a brief story about an experience I had on one of my first trips to Africa in this job.

I met a group of journalists who had fled a terror-ridden country—I am not going to name it in order to protect them—basically in fear for their lives. These guys were trained professionals. They were integrating into the country where they had taken refuge. And I asked them, so what is it like for you here? And they said, you know, we are happy to be here. We are happy to be safe, but every single one of us at some point has been arrested by the local police. Each time, they said, they had been held at the police station until a relative or friend could come to pay a bribe to get them out. One of them said the police station where we live, we do not actually call it a police station. We call it the people market.

Now, seeing as they had fled terrorism and obviously were on our side in this fight against terrorism, I asked them if someone they thought was a terrorist moved into their neighborhood, would they call the police. And they laughed. And one man replied, well, of course not. If we did that, either the police would come and arrest us again to get a bribe, or if they arrested the terrorist, someone would bribe him out and then he would come and kill us.

And so there I think in a nutshell is the connection between this scourge and our interest in fighting violent extremism around the world. No matter what else we do, we are not going to defeat that problem where there is no trust between governments and the communities where terrorists hide, where the authorities are as likely to shake people down as they are to protect them, where corruption hollows out security forces, where it feeds terrorist propaganda that promises to purify societies of this scourge.

And so fighting corruption is absolutely critical to our security. As Administrator Smith said, it is critical to a whole bunch of other important goals, including economic development. I would argue it is central as well to our promotion of human rights around the world, in part because corruption is the central organizing principle of a lot of dictatorships and—I think this is the interesting part— also often their biggest political vulnerability because stealing is in a sense the one crime that no dictator can ever justify and the one issue that is most likely to rally public support against them, as we have seen from Russia to Venezuela to many other countries.

So for these reasons, the administration has said that corruption has to be treated as a first order national security priority.

The question is how do you effectively combat something that is in many ways one of the oldest and deepest failures of human nature. And I think we have to be honest. We have not always been good at combating it, particularly when it exists at high levels, particularly when it is committed by people with great power, at least until those people have lost their power.

But I think we have an emerging strategy that can work. It begins by promoting greater transparency, which is something that we do throughout the world through international institutions like the G20, FATF, EITI. You mentioned the Dodd-Frank rule, which was an advance in that work. Because of this steady, slow, not dramatic work, it is much more likely today that the dirty money kleptocrats try to hide will come into the light.

Second, supporting civil society-led investigations. Greater transparency leaves the evidence of corruption hiding in plain sight, but someone still has to sort through the gigabytes of information that governments, companies, and financial institutions disclose to find it. And interestingly I think the transnational networks of journalists, NGOs have some advantages over government and law enforcement entities in finding the initial pieces of evidence that lead us to those crimes. And some of the work that we have mutually invested in with NGOs, just a few million dollars, has helped to spark seizures and settlements worth billions of dollars to our treasury and to other law-abiding governments around the world.

Third, we have got to support the law enforcement institutions because ultimately only they can prosecute the crime. One of our roles at the State Department is providing that kind of support with our colleagues in the Justice Department to emerging democracies that are asking us for help, Ukraine, Burma, Sri Lanka, Nigeria, and others. That is where we need resources. And where governments like that lack the will to act, that is where our own law enforcement agencies can step in and act, and we have seen the Justice Department through its new Anti-Kleptocracy Unit do some really remarkable and impactful things.

Now, across this range of efforts, there is more that needs to be done, and I will just mention a couple of things.

First, when I ask human rights activists around the world how the United States can best help them, they often say something like this. We know you do not control what happens in Russia or the Congo, but you do control what happens in America. So please, at the very least, do not let those who profit from abuse of power in our country hide their money in yours.

And yet, as you know, it is still possible for kleptocrats to establish anonymously owned shell companies in the United States. That is why we proposed legislation to require all companies formed in the U.S. to identify their so-called beneficial ownership, the actual human being who owns or controls them, and to make that information more readily available to law enforcement. There are few pieces of legislation Congress can pass that will do more to advance the fight against human rights abuses and corruption than this.

And we can provide more resources, particularly to the civil society organizations that expose the crime before anybody else does. At the London Summit on Anti-Corruption last month, Secretary Kerry announced that we will establish a global consortium to support the work of civil society and investigative journalists to uncover corruption around the world. We will be making an initial investment, but we hope that other governments, as well as private foundations, will contribute as well.

There is so much more we can talk about from using our visa authorities to better scrutiny of security assistance, to law enforcement cooperation mechanisms that we are trying to stand up. The goal here is to do for the anti-corruption movement what we did collectively for the human rights movement over the last 30 or 40 years, making it at that level in terms of global attention, that level in terms of how our foreign policy advances it. We are not there yet, but we are getting there. With your help, we will.

Thank you.

[Mr. Malinowski's prepared statement follows:]

PREPARED STATEMENT OF TOM MALINOWSKI

Chairman Corker, Ranking Member Cardin and members of the Committee, thank you for this opportunity to testify on the corrosive effects of corruption and kleptocracy and our efforts to combat them. We are grateful to the Committee for bringing increased attention to this challenge.

During one of my first visits to Africa in this job, I met a group of refugees who had fled a terror-ridden country on account of insecurity. They were trained professionals who had found work in their host country and were grateful for refuge, but when I asked what their new life was like, they noted treatment at the hands of the local police as one of the key challenges they continued to face. They each noted that they had been arrested at some point and held at the police station until a relative or friend could pay a bribe to get them out. One joked that they called the police station the "people market." Seeing as how they had fled terrorism, I asked whether they would call the police if someone they suspected of having terrorist links moved into their neighborhood. The group laughed, and one man replied: "Of course not. If we did that, either the police would arrest us again to get a bribe, or, if they arrested the terrorist, someone would bribe him out, and then he'd come to kill us."

Mr. Chairman, I have heard some version of this story again and again in every corner of the world. I think it illustrates well the connection on which you have asked us to focus today—between corruption and violent extremism.

Success in the fight against violent extremism depends in part on maintaining trust between governments and the communities where violent extremists hide and seek recruits. It can come down to whether people in those communities will call the police when they suspect trouble—to offer information or to ask for help. Corruption destroys that trust. When the authorities are as likely to shake people down as they are to protect them, people sometimes end up fearing the authorities more than the violent extremists. And some will be susceptible to terrorist propaganda that promises to purify their societies of this scourge.

As Secretary Kerry has said, there is no greater cause of disillusionment or surer way to alienate citizens from the state than the "sense that the system in rigged against them and that people in positions of power are crooks who steal the future of their own people." Terrorist groups from Nigeria to Iraq to Afghanistan have exploited such grievances to build support through promises of well-resourced, uncorrupt schools, hospitals, justice, security, and public services. And when these groups threaten the people and state, corruption inhibits the ability of the state to fight back. Where military and police promotions, equipment, and loyalties are sold to the highest bidder, security forces cannot fight effectively. When procurement systems are exploited, weapons end up on the black market. And when border guards can be bribed, terrorists travel freely along with illicit arms flows and human trafficking.

Fighting corruption is thus critical to our security. It's equally important to our shared prosperity. U.S. companies are disadvantaged by corrupt markets abroad, where they lose contracts to competitors that are willing to pay bribes. The World Bank estimates that approximately $1 trillion is paid every year in bribes by the private sector alone, enriching elites to the detriment of desperately needed public investments, from education to healthcare to food security.

Fighting corruption is also central to our promotion of human rights and democracy. I've long thought that corruption is the main organizing principle of the authoritarian states responsible for most human rights abuses, and most instability, in the world. The opportunity to profit from graft is the reason why many dictators seek and cling to power. Corruption gives them a means of purchasing loyalty—and a means of enforcing it, since everyone addicted to these ill-gotten gains has a stake in the regime's survival and anyone who breaks ranks can be selectively prosecuted.

At the same time—and here is where the opportunity lies—corruption can be an authoritarian government's greatest political vulnerability. Such governments can sometimes manufacture excuses for shooting demonstrators, arresting a critic, or censoring a newspaper but no cultural, patriotic, or national security argument can justify stealing. Anger over corruption helped inspire the uprisings of the Arab Spring. It is one of the central grievances of the movement to restore good governance to Venezuela. It is one reason why so many Africans don't want their leaders to stay in power for life. It is the cause around which the most effective opponents of Putinism in Russia rally. Dictators see this, and they are becoming increasingly ruthless in silencing those who tell the truth about corruption; some of the human rights activists we work hardest to protect are those threatened for reporting on bribery, kickbacks, and the movement of illicit funds across borders. But it is becoming harder and harder to hide corruption, and that is a ray of hope for those struggling for more democratic governance around the world, at a moment when such hope is greatly needed.

For all these reasons, the 2015 National Security Strategy included corruption as a global concern and likewise through the QDDR and other policies, Secretary Kerry has insisted that we treat corruption as a first order national security priority. With our colleagues at the White House, Treasury, Justice, and USAID, the State Department has made a concerted push to combat corruption. Our comprehensive, whole-of-government approach is committed to supporting government reformers and civil society actors who hold leaders and institutions accountable and to strengthening international norms against corruption. For example by promoting Goal 16 of the Sustainable Development Goals; and leading by example to further strengthen our own anti-corruption efforts by putting forward wide-ranging commitments at the UK Anti-Corruption Summit last month.

A Three-Pronged Approach

Over the last several years, independent civil society-led investigations supported by the State Department's Bureau for Democracy, Rights, and Labor (DRL) and

USAID have steadily worked to reveal instances of massive corruption involving foreign companies and foreign officials in their communities, and to report on law enforcement actions taken abroad against such officials and those who would corrupt them. By exposing corrupt conduct at home, civil society has provided important leads to domestic and foreign law enforcement and increased the impact of successful criminal investigations. The Justice Department—and, increasingly, other law enforcement authorities around the world—have launched their own probes that have resulted in billions of dollars in fines being levied against bribe payers and millions of dollars in recoveries from foreign kleptocrats for the benefit of the people harmed by the abuse of public office.

For just a few million dollars in U.S. support for civil society, this approach represents a good return on investment and an important element of a broader, effective strategy to combat grand corruption.

That strategy begins by promoting greater transparency globally and domestically and supporting multilateral anti-corruption initiatives. Law enforcement investigations like those I described have become more successful in part because of reforms the United States has promoted through the G-20, the United Nations Convention Against Corruption, the Financial Action Task Force (FATF), the Extractive Industries Transparency Initiative, and other institutions to increase the transparency of banking transactions, company records, extractive industry payments to governments, and the assets of public officials. The Bureau for International Law and Narcotics' Anti-Corruption team is at negotiating tables around the world to ensure these standards are continuously strengthened. Greater transparency and accountability also empowers civil society to expose corruption affecting their own communities. In 2011, President Obama launched the Open Government Partnership with seven world leaders to encourage governments in partnership with civil society to advance transparency and accountability through national action plans for reform. Seventy countries now participate in the Partnership and are subject to independent review every two years. In addition to implementing our own action plan at home, the United States supports efforts to help other countries join OGP and assists with the implementation of their action plans. We are working to improve transparency in the extractive sectors by supporting the Extractive Industries Transparency Initiative globally and, under the leadership of the Department of the Interior, within the United States through a multi-stakeholder group that brings together companies, state and tribal governments, and civil society. The SEC's issuance this week of a final rule implementing Section 1504 of the Dodd-Frank Wall Street Reform and Consumer Protection Act strengthens our credibility on corruption and transparency internationally.

Second, we need to support civil society-led investigations. Greater transparency leaves evidence of corruption hiding in plain sight, but someone still has to sort through the gigabytes of information that governments, companies, and financial institutions disclose each day to find it. Transnational networks of journalists and non-governmental organizations like those that have recently reported on notorious examples of kleptocracy can effectively advance this work through a combination of local knowledge and relationships with counterparts in other countries. Journalists and NGO networks are often the first to uncover illicit activity because they can deploy researchers in multiple countries at once, and because they tend to have anonymous sources who provide them with information, key documents, or road maps for how to obtain them. By exposing suspect conduct, journalists and NGOs have sparked further investigation by law enforcement authorities or enabled financial institutions to better scrutinize the accounts of their clients.

Third, we need to support effective law enforcement. Ultimately, corruption is a crime committed by powerful people accustomed to impunity. While non-governmental networks can expose suspect activity, only governments can prosecute it. Furthermore, civil society often lacks the access to financial and other protected information available to law enforcement.

Wherever possible, we should invest in the capacity of governments with the will to be part of the solution, and this is a role that the State Department in particular, working in coordination and in conjunction with USAID and the Justice Department, can play. It is especially important that we coordinate and provide such support quickly to countries where reformers have come to power and have asked our help to strengthen institutions or to bring corrupt actors to justice and to recover their assets. A good example is Burma, where the success of a historic democratic transition will depend in part on whether the new government can get control of natural resource revenues that in the past have disappeared from public accounts. We are ramping up our support to the government and civil society to help. Kenya is another: a key outcome of President Obama's visit there was a joint commitment on good governance and anticorruption in which our two countries promised to work together on everything from ethics training to procurement reform to police account-ability. A third is Nigeria, where we are providing a variety of assistance to the government's Economic and Financial Crimes Commission and working to deepen our collaboration on asset recovery. We have many other opportunities to engage such governments in 2016—for example in Sri Lanka, Tunisia, Guatemala, Mozambique, and Burkina Faso.

And where governments lack the will to act, and funds connected to illicit activities touch the U.S. financial system, our own law enforcement institutions can play a key role. The Justice Department established a Kleptocracy Unit in 2010, which has taken on cases including the recovery of assets stolen by the late Nigerian Head of State Sani Abacha and his associates, to funds misappropriated by the Second Vice President of Equatorial Guinea Teodoro Nguema Obiang, and corrupt monies tied to the former head of the Department of Health and Social Security in Honduras. The Justice Department Fraud Section's Foreign Corrupt Practices Act Unit criminally prosecutes those individuals and companies over which the United States has jurisdiction who pay bribes to foreign corrupt officials. And the FBI recently established three International Corruption Squads to investigate and prosecute such foreign corruption. They could do even more with greater capacity and by strengthening legal authorities to combat kleptocracy.

Current Efforts

Across this range of efforts, there is more to be done.

For example, while we have done a great deal to promote financial transparency around the world, we still have work to do at home. When I ask human rights activists around the world how the United States can best help them, they often say something like: "We know you don't control what happens in Russia or the Congo, but you do control what happens in America. So please, at the very least, don't let those who profit from abuse of power in our country to hide their money in yours."

And yet, as you know Mr. Chairman, it is still possible for kleptocrats and those who seek to hide their wealth from around the world, and criminals of every other sort, to establish anonymously owned shell companies in the United States, and to use them to stash their illicitly acquired wealth in banks all over the world. That's why the Obama administration is proposing legislation to require all companies formed in the United States to identify their "beneficial ownership"—the actual human beings who own or control them—to the Department of the Treasury and make that information more readily available to law enforcement. There are few pieces of legislation that Congress can pass this year that will do more to advance the cause of global human rights and anti-corruption, and I hope Congress will act.

The successes of the Department of Justice's Kleptocracy Asset Recovery Initiative are mostly achieved through civil forfeiture actions. Preserving and strengthening that authority will be instrumental to the success of U.S. efforts to combat kleptocracy going forward. U.S. law enforcement could be strengthened through additional legislative steps to enhance the Department of Justice's ability to prevent bad actors from concealing and laundering illegal proceeds of transnational corruption and allow U.S. prosecutors to more effectively pursue such cases.

We can also do more to support the civil society groups that uncover evidence of corruption as more information about kleptocrats' finances becomes available. Efforts supported by DRL at the State Department have demonstrated the potential of this work. When a DRL-USAID funded investigative media organization uncovered a $20 billion money laundering operation that funneled money from Russia through Moldovan courts to Latvia and the UK, a local investigation revealed that a Latvian bank was the destination for many of these funds. Latvian regulators asked the European Central Bank to revoke the bank's license, and it did. In Central America, two journalists we supported revealed the embezzlement of millions of dollars by the mayor of a Guatemalan town. The story was quickly picked up by several media organizations, eventually prompting an investigation that resulted in the now former mayor's disqualification from the 2015 elections. In Kyrgyzstan, when an investigative media story developed as part of a DRL grant revealed $200,000 in funding embezzled by a local official, the resulting outcry prompted local law enforcement to launch an official investigation.

To build on this work, we announced at the UK Anti-Corruption Summit that State would establish a Global Consortium with USAID support to support the work of civil society and investigative journalists to uncover corruption. We will be making an initial investment in the Consortium, and hope that other governments as well as private foundations will contribute as well.

Asset recovery, essential to our international commitment to return stolen assets for the benefit of the people harmed by corruption, will be strengthened by the United States commitment to cohost in 2017 the first meeting of a Global Forum on Asset Recovery, a new mechanism to work collaboratively on major asset recovery cases where there is emergent need, modeled after the successful Ukraine and Arab Forums on Asset Recovery. With an initial focus on Nigeria, Sri Lanka, Tunisia, and Ukraine, this Forum will support law enforcement and civil society efforts in these countries while also providing a key way to reinforce the capacity of reform-minded governments with political will.

At the State Department, we can reinforce these efforts through responsible, effective implementation of the visa restriction for kleptocrats and by ensuring that U.S. foreign assistance discourages rather than inadvertently fuels corruption. In London, the United States committed to integrate anti-corruption intro training for foreign security forces, ensure that our security assistance works to improve governance, and better assesses risk of corruption throughout our cooperation with foreign security forces. We are encouraged by the strong support of allies at the Department of Defense on these efforts and know there is more we can do.

Conclusion

Across all of these efforts, Congressional support will be vital to strong and effective follow through. None of this will be easy. Recent headlines have revealed the pervasiveness of global corruption and the deep web of laws, practice, and systems that will need to change—much bigger than any one law firm—to root it out. But this effort also reflects the growing capacity and will of those who demand accountability and expose the truth. We will not rid the world of dishonesty and greed, but we can realistically hope to empower willing reformers to set their countries on a new path, and to increase the likelihood that kleptocracy is exposed and punished—not just years after the fact but when the officials involved are still in power. And if we can make powerful leaders think twice before accepting a bribe or demanding a kickback or hiding their wealth in a shell company, if we can enforce the law at the highest levels and disrupt illicit supply chains, we strengthen our efforts to tackle the lower level corruption of police officers and petty civil servants that bedevils ordinary people, makes them more susceptible to violent extremism, and undermines democratic governance and security in so many countries.

Just as, over the last half century, the human rights movement took human rights from the periphery of international relations to a core policy concern—to ensure global security and the protection of universal values—our goal is to make anti-corruption a similar international priority today.

Thank you for the opportunity to testify today and for your partnership in the hard work ahead. I look forward to any questions.

The CHAIRMAN. Well, thank you very much for that testimony. I appreciate the suggestion as to what we can do better here.

And along that line, Ben and I were over this morning, as he mentioned, at the TIP release and saw the inspirational work of people in other countries that risk their lives to help other people relative to slavery. And I look at all the things—I know in this political season, there is a lot of discussion about how bad our country is, but our country does a lot of great things around the world with very little resources in most cases. You know, I think sometimes we do not talk enough about that and what it means to other people who are victims or have difficult circumstances for us to show that leadership.

At the same time, to you, Administrator Smith, we have begun to look a lot at what we do at USAID. I know we have not had an authorization in years for lots of reasons. And it seems like that we do an outstanding job in the health care area. It is amazing what our Nation has done relatively to HIV and what people collectively have done with malaria and tuberculosis. It is pretty amazing. And it seems like we can do a lot on the economic front with a different focus.

But a lot of people look at what we ourselves do as sort of a holdover from the Cold War model where much of our foreign aid is really about buying influence and we have not really transitioned to a place that is more beneficial than it could be.

Are there things that we could look at within our own aid assistance to move away from, again, a Cold War model where we are competing against the Soviet Union for influence? Is that one of the issues that we have, that in essence, we still carry out aid in that manner? And are we in some cases actually allowing more corruption to take place in countries?

Ms. SMITH. Thank you for that question, Senator.

There is always more that we can do. I would point to a few things.

You rightly said at the beginning that we do a lot around the world and we sometimes do not tell our story very well. I actually think our story on this issue is one that we do not tell as we might because one of the things that matters is the standards that we uphold. So, for example, the recent SEC ruling puts us in very good stead and gives us at USAID and also the State Department a better foundation upon which to stand.

We have found that in a number of countries—I met with leaders recently of Guatemala, Ukraine, Georgia, and Albania. All of them raised corruption and what they wanted to do and had done about corruption, wanted to do with us about corruption from the outset. I think in those cases, one of the things that would be very helpful that we could do together is elevate more frequently and more visibly the examples of countries and/or leaders who are taking often bold and courageous steps to fight corruption because it is often at great political risk. Now, all of those countries face huge challenges, may succeed, may fail, but I think giving them visibility when they try.

Something that is helping us I think get over the hurdle that you point to—and I think we are certainly further along than we were during the Cold War. Two things I think for USAID.

One is identifying cases even in those countries where we may have a major national security priority and a number of interests at play where we can pull whatever thread we need to pull to start to make progress on corruption. I am reasonably optimistic about some of the threads we have been able to identify recently, for example, in places like Afghanistan.

But the second is the work that we do on evaluation because I think that is the work that tells us where we are making progress and where we are not. We do 200 of those a year. We publish them. I think that is the evidence base that can help us from a policy perspective and a programming perspective be frank about what we know about what is working and what is not because that is part of what we got to grapple with.

The CHAIRMAN. Again, back to the essence of the question, we dole out just lots of resources and programs that are just redundant all around the world that are not really what you would call— they are not breakthrough kinds of things. You know, people expect it. They know it is going to come. Again, as you know, I mean, I am a strong supporter of our engagement around the world and am just so proud of what our Nation has done to deal with HIV and what we are getting ready to do, I hope, to deal with modern slavery. So please know I am a strong supporter of those efforts.

But when I travel around the world, as all of us do, and I look at these over and over and over programs that are having no effect really and that these governments just expect that these monies are going to come regardless of their actions, are we really—just with the way we pass out monies in ways that—with definitions that sound great, but are we really doing what we should in the deliverance of aid to ensure that we are not contributing more so to corruption in the countries? I know we are evaluating. I know we are holding up heroes. But have we ever looked at the way we are delivering aid to more fully empower people within those countries that are doing the right things versus many of the governments that we deal with that are not?

Ms. SMITH. I think that is a good question. I would point to a couple things we are doing. I think having support from you all up here on those would be helpful.

And one point I would make is that from the USAID side, we provide very little money directly to governments, very, very little money, and where we do provide money to a government as in through a government's budget, it is for a project-specific, time-defined period. And we report to Congress on those, and there is a lot of work that goes in on the front end to assess risk.

The other thing that we have been doing for a few years is what we call selectivity and focus where we really look at our programs around the world and using these evaluations to judge in part what is not working. What are the things we have been doing for 10, 12, 15 years that we just do because it is automatic, and where and how do we stop those? There have been more than 200 programs curtailed by AID over the last few years, and there are many countries we are looking at where it is our view that we should either scale back or pull out altogether. So that is part of the regular process within USAID right now, and it would be great to have support for our doing that on a regular basis and for you to take a look at that and see if you are in agreement of where we are making those choices.

The CHAIRMAN. That would be good.

Listen, Senator Menendez I know has a time issue, and we are glad to defer to him.

Senator MENENDEZ. Thank you, Mr. Chairman, and I thank the ranking member for his courtesy.

Thank you both for your work.

Let me ask you. With reference to Afghanistan, which is constantly ranked one of the top three most corrupt countries in the world behind North Korea and Somalia, on April 28th of this year, the Senate passed the Afghanistan Accountability Act. And I am proud to have worked with the chairman and the ranking member to have been an author of it. It provides for the President to offer technical and financial assistance to the Government of Afghanistan and Afghan civil society. And while it is early, I wonder how you can measure our progress in addressing corruption in Afghanistan since we have committed so many lives and national treasure to that country.

I understand that President Ghani has made a significant commitment to addressing corruption, but he is only one person. How would you assess the Afghan Government's commitment across the board?

Ms. SMITH. Thank you, Senator, and thank you also for your work on this issue of accountability. We think it is critically important not in the least because we are responsible for taxpayer dollars, but it is also the thing that determines whether we have the outcomes we are trying to achieve.

I would say it is too early to tell whether across the board the government has institutionalized and internalized the commitment that President Ghani has made.

But part of our job is to try to find ways to make these things work. So let me tell you about a meeting I recently had with Afghanistan's minister of health. He recently commissioned an evaluation of the entire health sector through their monitoring and evaluation committee that the president stood up on corruption, to identify cases of corruption across the health sector. As you might expect, it was a fairly damning report that identified a huge amount of corruption across the system from procurement to local officials, all the way through. He is now—and we will work with him to do this—putting together a plan to take on those gaps step by step by step.

Now, is that enough to reverse the situation in Afghanistan altogether or to take it from the corrupt side of the ledger and put it in the non-corrupt side? No. It is an opportunity, though—and this is something we have seen in development across the board—to demonstrate what can be done such that others have the incentive or in some cases the obligation and the pressure from civil society to replicate.

So, again, it is small but we think it is not insignificant. I think this will be a good measure of whether the government is, in fact, internalizing the kind of directives that President Ghani has put forward. And we are happy to keep you informed of it as it unfolds.

Senator MENENDEZ. I would be interested in knowing. I understand that the Afghan Government has made efforts to diminish, for example, corruption at border and customs posts.

Ms. SMITH. Yes.

Senator MENENDEZ. And that progress should be recognized and commended at the same time that we are urging them to do other things.

But I am wondering, Secretary Malinowski, whether—our legislation suggested that individual Afghan Government officials should be subject to visa bans and asset freezes in the event they are found to be involved in the type of corruption that we are talking about. Similar measures have been taken in the cases of Russia and Hungary. Are those efforts efforts that are warranted in this regard? We want to see what President Ghani is doing in our assistance, as Administrator Smith talked about in the health care, but when there is a reticence to move, are we going to consider those types of actions?

Mr. MALINOWSKI. I think as a general rule we would agree that you need a combination of capacity building for those who are committed to being part of the solution, and there are many people in Afghanistan who are passionately committed to this because it is their country and they do not want their country sold to the highest bidder, and I think President Ghani is the first among them but a combination of that capacity building and accountability.

We have, as you know, visa ban authority related to corruption. The evidentiary standard, as I have learned in my 2 years in this job, is quite high, I would say appropriately high when you are using those kinds of tools, as it is for asset freezes, financial sanctions, and the things that Treasury and DOJ do very effectively.

But there is certainly no reticence when it comes to using those authorities. We have used them all over the world. When we deny a visa or simply put someone on a watch list because they have not applied yet, it is not something that people generally know except for the person who may walk into an embassy and apply for a visa and realize that there is a problem.

Senator MENENDEZ. But it is a powerful message when it is appropriately used, and that message spreads as we say in Spanish radio bemba, which means, you know, radio lips. It spreads really quick in terms of the consequences and that we are serious about it. I do not suggest that we use it carte blanche, but when it is appropriate, if you use it, I think it has a ripple effect along the way.

May I have one last question, if I may?

Mr. Gershman, who is on the next panel—and I have a great deal of respect for him and the work that they do—has in is testimony something that I just think we should call attention to because I did not even really think about it. In a sense, I know it, but I really did not think about it. He calls it the problem of Western enablers, basically entities in the West that ultimately help take those entities in the world, those individuals in the world who ultimately use the ill-gotten gains in a way and cleanse it so that they can become philanthropists to get, in his own remarks, photographed alongside celebrated international figures and media stars.

I am wondering—and this may be not a State Department issue. It may be a different dimension, Mr. Chairman, of our work here. But I am wondering what we do—and the ranking member—to think about how we can create some type of effort to suggest that if you knowingly engage in the practice of helping people cleanse their ill-gotten gains, it may not be through the banking system, although the banking system may be one of them, one of the most powerful elements of it, but in other ways as well that there is some type of action to be considered because if you cannot cleanse your money and you are stuck where you are and you want to really get out or you want to protect your money somewhere else and have access to what it means and it gets closed down, it is another element I think globally of trying to pursue it. So I just think it is a tremendous part of Mr. Gershman's testimony that struck me, and I just wanted to bring it up as food for thought.

The CHAIRMAN. I do not want to condemn everybody that is in this program by any stretch, but that is one of the concerns I have had about the EB–5 program, candidly, you know, where people are buying the ability to live here in our country with large sums of money. I would say the vast majority of people who do so are probably fine people, but my guess is there are a whole lot of folks that are not in that category and we are actually encouraging that. I appreciate the legislation you suggested a minute ago.

Senator MENENDEZ. And how we vet, whether for that program or others, is a real concern. I share your interest.

Thank you.

The CHAIRMAN. Did you want to say something?

Ms. SMITH. Just two quick things on this. I think you are right that other agencies and departments are very focused on this, including Treasury and Justice, because they have been scrutinizing things like high-end real estate and other things that people are able to do to use ill-gotten gains to establish themselves here or elsewhere.

I would just make a brief plug for something else which is related to this but I think would help, which we started working on several years ago and Secretary Kerry announced that the U.S. and the U.K. will convene a global forum on asset recovery because part of the challenge here is that we know that these kleptocrats steal billions of dollars. It is hard to then get a hold of that money and reinvest it in development or anything else. We have tried to streamline our procedures and those of other countries so it is easier for citizens to track down those assets, but I think this is an area where the U.S. can continue to lead. It does not entirely solve the problem you point to, but it does send a signal that we are better and better at and will come after your assets, which is a good disincentive.

Senator MENENDEZ. Thank you, Mr. Chairman.

The CHAIRMAN. Senator Perdue?

Senator PERDUE. Thank you.

And thank you both for being here.

I just want to thank the ranking member and the chairman for having this meeting. I think a lot of people look at the title of this and say, well, okay, it is another hearing. This is a profound hearing in my view because of the situation we are in the world. I would like to put a little perspective on that.

Right now, in 1992 to 2000 under President Clinton, the State Department spent about $20 billion running itself, and it was very consistent, $20 billion a year. Under President Bush, we averaged about $30 billion, and that includes USAID. In the last 7 years, we have spent $54 billion. Of that, $34 billion has been pretty routinely spent on foreign aid. And when I look at that and look at the comparative balance of what we have been borrowing in the last 7 years, compare that with the percentage that is discretionary—this comes out of our discretionary budget. These are dollars we argue about every year. About 30 percent of what we spend is discretionary. But we are borrowing 35 percent, which means that every dollar that we spend, the discretionary, including USAID money, is technically borrowed money. And let me say that again, Mr. Chairman. Technically every dime we spend on defense, every dime we spend on foreign aid, and a lot of what we spend on domestic programs is borrowed. Therefore, it behooves us to be very, very careful about how we invest this money.

That does not mean that we are not all very, very strong supporters of the impact of our foreign aid. We have reduced through the Marshall Plan, foreign aid, and a lot of other things, globalization and our own economy—we have reduced poverty in the rest of the world dramatically in the last 50 years, while our poverty since 1965 remains pretty much unchanged.

So I think this puts in perspective why this is so—this anti-corruption issue is so important and how we spend our money here is so important.

I am an advocate that we actually need to spend more. I think we could avoid wars and all that. You have heard me talk about that. But I love the leverage impact of what you guys are already doing with Power Africa and others where we get private money to partner with public money and actually get great economic returns.

However, people like General Kelly, the former combat commander of SOUTHCOM, whose primary responsibility was to interdict drugs coming in the United States, says because of limited resources, he can only really interdict about 20 percent of what they actually see and can measure. So this is the comparison of priorities.

And I know that what you do, Ms. Smith, since you have been there—you have only been there a little while—is to focus on priorities. You have talked to me about that. I have heard you talk publicly about that. I would love to have you talk about that relative to the issues here.

But let me put one last point of perspective. We spend about $34 billion in foreign aid. There are only about 75 of the world's largest companies whose revenue is bigger than that. So if you think about it, Delta Airlines, a pretty big outfit—Delta Airlines in my home State, if you took all of their revenues, it would equate pretty much to what we spend in foreign aid. That puts it in perspective. But I would love to know of that, what percentage do we think is being siphoned off through corrupt practices in places that we are trying to help. And we know that there is some percentage. And what percentage are we spending of the $34 billion toward anti-corruption efforts? Those are two questions.

And then I guess the other is the chairman mentioned redundant. I know you have a heart about this. Programs that are similar, programs that are redundant—give us an idea. You have only been on the ground a little while. Tell us your early opinion about that as well, if you do not mind.

Ms. SMITH. About redundancy.

Senator PERDUE. Redundancy.

Ms. SMITH. Thank you, Senator. Let me say a couple things.

In terms of where this fits in priorities, I would say it is a very high priority, the whole issue of anti-corruption. The way that is manifested is actually quite interesting I think. AID did a study looking at 300 anti-corruption programs between 2008 and 2013 to determine their effectiveness. And what was concluded—and I think it is right—was that we would have greater impact if we integrate this as much as possible into everything we do as opposed to just having a little subset of anti-corruption programs over here.

So the way we actually spend our money—we have some resources that go to dedicated anti-corruption programs. It may be supporting a commission of integrity, training, specific support for civil society on that. But our other resources, for example, that I think are having a huge impact—one, as both Tom and I have talked about, is ongoing support for civil society, which enables it not only to incrementally and incidentally take on corruption, but in the big picture if you look at Guatemala or Ukraine, the changes in public citizens' demands in those countries had a lot to do with the strength of civil society over time.

Senator PERDUE. What rough percentage, just directionally, would you say that we are spending in this anti-corruption effort?

Ms. SMITH. If it is specific anti-corruption, it is in the range of $70 million to $80 million. But let me give you another example, Ukraine, where it has been a huge concern of all of us. We have helped Ukraine put in place an electronic procurement system, not the most sexy development bumper sticker we can put out there, but the impact of that is huge because it reduces the number of people in a transaction. It makes the information transparent and available to everybody to look at the entire system, and it has a huge impact on the ability of people to exploit the system. We do not count those dollars as corruption dollars. They are part of the broader Ukraine package. So I am hesitant to say it is this much money in a given case, the work we have done on customs and border control and training and that kind of issue.

I think in terms of what is siphoned off, let me state a couple things at the outset. We are constantly looking at where we are vulnerable. One of the things I am very pleased about is the committee, at about the same time you confirmed me, you confirmed a new inspector general who has been enormously effective and we work very closely with. We frequently ask her and her team to look into things and give us recommendations on how we improve.

I have made very clear that that is something we got to do on a regular basis because we are never going to get to the point where I can say we have no vulnerabilities, nothing is being siphoned off. We have got to constantly work at that.

I am impressed with the measures USAID has put in place over the last several years, whether it is the upfront risk assessments, the training that we are now doing for our people, the training that we have started and intend to expand for our implementers on anti-corruption and programming and project design. I think we have got a number of safeguards. We face the biggest challenge in places where we have got ongoing crisis or conflict, large sums of money, and security conditions mean that we do not have the kind of physical access we might have in some other cases. So we are doubling down on those.

But I would say—and I have known this agency for a long time, as you and I have discussed—it is a long stronger and a lot better on this than it was a few years ago. But I would also say we have got to do that on an iterative, constant basis to make sure we are checking for loopholes and vulnerabilities wherever they may be.

Senator PERDUE. Thank you.

The CHAIRMAN. Mr. Malinowski?

Mr. MALINOWSKI. Thanks.

I would add that embedded in the excellent question that you asked and Administrator Smith's answer is the insight that the small amounts of money that we do spend on anti-corruption, if it is well spent, saves a lot of money.

Let me give you another example, a country many of us have followed and been interested in for a long time and that is Burma. For 25 years, through various means, we were trying to promote a democratic transition in that country supporting Aung San Suu Kyi and the brave democrats who were fighting for their liberation of their country. And this year, she becomes the leader of the country after a free election. And her first duty is to now try to deliver for her people economic dividends, making their lives better. And obviously, we want to help.

Now, how can we do that? One way would be to find billions of dollars of foreign assistance, channel it in there through the World Bank and through our own budget. We do not have that.

But it also happens to turn out that this is a wealthy country. They have got immense natural resources, and they have been siphoning off billions every single year, particularly in this case from jade mining, which is one of their most lucrative natural resource industries, literally billions of dollars a year through corruption and mismanagement, all of that empowering the old forces, the military, the kind of military crony complex that used to run the country.

So actually just helping them get budgetary transparency, just helping them figure out where the money is going, helping civil society in Burma, as you mentioned, track this stuff and uncover the corruption that still exists, which we can do for much less money, can have an enormous dividend for that country and for our interests. And so replicating that across the board is what we are trying to be about.

Senator PERDUE. Thank you.

Thank you, Mr. Chairman.

The CHAIRMAN. If I could before turning to Senator Cardin. This comes out of the QDDR at the State Department, just to put an exclamation point on this last conversation. This is worldwide. The annual cost to end world hunger is $30 billion. Official development assistance around the world—around the world—is $134 billion. Annual investment needed to achieve universal mobile broadband service around the world, connectivity everywhere, $168 billion. I am going to skip over to the total number—the total amount of bribes paid, $1 trillion. $1 trillion. The total cost of corruption, $2.6 trillion worldwide.

And so when we look at those areas where we can make a difference, whether it is ending modern slavery or dealing with HIV or dealing with other things, this certainly is an area, certainly difficult to deal with worldwide—and I know you are all working on it on a daily basis—but where a huge impact could take place.

With that, Senator Cardin.

Senator CARDIN. Well, Mr. Chairman, thank you for bringing up those dollars.

And, Senator Perdue, you are right on target with the question, and I very much respect the answers that we have received. But if you look at the total resources being devoted here directly, it is extremely small, and indirectly it is still very small. The dollars that we put into specific missions, whether it be hunger or health, are very, very important. Do not get me wrong. But they overshadow all the other funds that are available within development assistance to help other countries. And if you look at the basic programs that have existed for a long time, not the new commitments we made within the last decade, it has not grown at all. So we are being outmatched when you look at what is at stake on the other side of the criminal elements in order to be able to continue their investments.

Secretary Malinowski, I very much appreciated the way you connected the dots. We all understand that it is difficult to get communities to cooperate with law enforcement to deal with extremists in their community. It is difficult under ideal circumstances. It is difficult in America. But when you add the corruption of the local police officer, it is impossible. So it does fuel terrorism. And thank you for connecting the dots there.

I certainly support the administration's efforts for disclosure on shell corporations. I think it is totally consistent with what Congress did on Magnitsky. We want to deny these corrupt officials the ability to hide their resources in the United States. That is where they want to hide them. And disclosure on the shell companies would help.

So I want to sort of use one of the procedures we use in order to make progress, and that is we try to promote best practices. Take what has worked and invest in that again. In trafficking in persons, we know what has worked. We had a lot of programs to deal with human trafficking, but we spotlighted one in the Trafficking in Persons Report that was passed by Congress so that we could have a common bible on accountability, on mission in each specific country, and it would not only help the U.S. direct efforts but would help the civil societies in the world effort to combat human trafficking.

And then a second issue that Senator Corker brought to our attention that is now working through our process—it was his leadership—to engage civil society is by putting legislation in that allowed us to leverage our dollars to get more civil participation in trafficking.

So in both cases, I think we could do much better on corruption. So we are looking at legislation that would do a trafficking in persons-type report for corruption so that we could have a common barometer globally of what we expect countries to put in place to deal with corruption, that they have the anti-corruption laws, that they have prosecutors, that they have the resources put out, those types of issues, and then evaluating these countries so that we can try to make the same type of progress that we have made in trafficking.

And then the second point, as I mentioned, about Senator Corker's bill that is making its way through the Congress that would allow us to leverage our dollars to get civil societies greater opportunity to make advancements on fighting corruption.

So do I get your endorsement on these two bills? [Laughter.]

Mr. MALINOWSKI. Thank you for that.

And I think both of us have acknowledged that we are not doing enough yet. I think we are proud of what we are doing. We are not yet where we need to be. And there are definitely areas where both greater resources, greater authorities, and in some cases greater direction from the Congress would be helpful. And so I can sincerely say we welcome legislation and we want to make with you to make sure that it is going to be, in fact, helpful.

Senator CARDIN. But rather than reinventing the wheel, why do we not just take the model that was used in trafficking?

Mr. MALINOWSKI. And you and I have discussed this, and I tried to be honest in talking about what I think are our strengths and our weaknesses as an institution. And I think as I have suggested, it is easier for us to go to a foreign government, to sit with the foreign leader, look them in the eye, and evaluate their efforts on trafficking than it is to grade them as the United States on their own criminality, which is what corruption is. I am not saying it should not be done. I am just saying it is a slightly different matter to look a foreign leader in the face and say you are accepting bribes or you are not doing enough to root out criminality from your own institution.

I will tell you what we do do and probably could do better is in the whole range of reporting that we already do on anti-corruption—we looked at this. We have a whole bunch of reports that touch on different pieces of this. We have got the human rights report, which my bureau puts out, which now includes reporting on corruption. We have got the IAGGA report, the International Anti-Corruption and Good Governance report which our INL Bureau puts out only a handful of countries, which is I think the closest to what you are looking for.

We could, I think, conceivably consolidate a lot of that reporting into a single transparent, online, public platform where we would also take in reporting and evaluations from the World Bank, from other international institutions so that it is all in one place. I actually think it is more effective if we build in international indicators because then it is not just the United States telling other countries what their grade is, which is sometimes useful but sometimes leads to problems.

So I think we can get there. We can work on something here that will achieve the purpose that I think you are looking for.

Senator CARDIN. I absolutely will follow up on everything you just said. I would just point out in rebuttal for one moment Ukraine is a country that is challenged on corruption. We have said that publicly. Our government has said that publicly. And the Ukrainians have accepted our analysis. It is not condemning their leaders for being corrupt. It is a country that has corruption in its core. Many of the Central American countries, which are democracies, have real huge corruption issues with extortion and drug trafficking. We know that. So I am not so sure if a country is on a path to try to deal with it, they are not helped by the analysis that we could give to bolster their need to make the type of changes that their country needs.

Mr. MALINOWSKI. And I will agree with that. And we do. And we do put out assessments, as you just noted. And we put them out in a way that is not consolidated, as I have conceded, and I think that is something that we can work on together.

Senator CARDIN. Thank you.

The CHAIRMAN. Go ahead, Gayle.

Ms. SMITH. Just a couple things. I would agree with what has been said. I think we can look at ways to pull some of these reports together, but also using the international monitoring that is done, there are a lot of countries that care what their transparency international rating is, and I think we should take advantage of that rather than potentially replicate that. I do not think that is what you are suggesting.

But if I could just say something about—you talked about what works and what would we actually look at and just offer a couple thoughts on that because we look a lot at that in terms of how we measure the success we are making.

One is obviously transparency and whether a country publishes its budget. The civil society role in this—it has to do with their civil society law, the ability of civil society to avail itself of a freedom of information act and otherwise organize.

This issue of systems and institutions—it is not something we typically look at, but you referred in your opening comments I believe to customs and border controls, procurement systems. That is the architecture of a state, and that is the machinery through which criminals operate, corrupt officials operate, and terrorists operate.

But I also think we should measure progress because one of the things we have learned across the board in development is that we are getting a lot of traction where countries are mimicking success that they see elsewhere. So if we can highlight cases where we are seeing more progress, I think that would be useful.

And finally, Senator Corker, I think your points are absolutely on board when you look at the numbers. And I often think of looking at the resources that could be regained by success against corruption is development financing. And I think that is how we should frame it, that this is potential financing for development. But I would not put anti-corruption and health in two different baskets. I will just give you a brief example.

In the Dominican Republic, as part of our health work on strengthening their health system, we did a review with them of their payroll system. 3,900 ghost workers were identified. They were summarily eliminated. They did not exist in the first place. It is a savings of $9 million a year that they are reinvesting in the health sector.

So we have got tangible examples of this being development financing, but I think also of our ability in sectors where the headline may be global health to again do that systems scrub to make sure we are fighting corruption even in those areas.

The CHAIRMAN. Thank you.

Senator Rubio?

Senator RUBIO. Thank you.

Secretary Malinowski, we have on numerous occasions passed different tools now available to the administration. For example, the Venezuela Defense of Human Rights and Civil Society Act that we are trying to get reauthorized gives the administration the power to punish human rights abusers and those involved in corruption.

So in Venezuela, the principal henchmen backing the autocratic Maduro regime, according to multiple published sources—everybody knows it. It is one of those things everybody knows—are cocaine smugglers. They are money launderers. For example, Diosdado Cabello, one of the leaders in the majority party—I guess the minority party now, but Maduro's party—Tarek El Aissami.

And there are just dozens of security officials and political leaders who are being investigated for this, not to mention dozens more of Venezuelan officials who have looted state-run enterprises, manipulated currency for their own pocketbook, and stealing from the people of this country while people are roaming the streets looking for food.

Why have Cabello or El Aissami or any of these other thugs not—why have these top-notch, high level people not been sanctioned?

Mr. MALINOWSKI. First of all, I agree with your assessment, and I agree that in many cases, even if we are looking at Venezuela as a human rights challenge or a democracy challenge, that coming at it from the standpoint of anti-corruption is both the right thing to do and a very effective thing to do because, as I mentioned in my opening statement, stealing is the one thing you cannot justify in any political context no matter what your propaganda or ideology or support base. Nobody can justify it.

And so we have imposed sanctions on a number, as you know, of Venezuelan officials. In terms of visa bans, I think we are up to about 62 Venezuelans. Most of this we do not name because of the way in which our visa ban authorities are structured. But I can tell you that from my standpoint, having looked at who is responsible for some of the things that you just mentioned, we have captured virtually everybody against whom we have decent evidence of corruption, human rights abuses, including at a very high level. In fact, just yesterday I signed out a few more. So we should be——

Senator RUBIO. Well, again, I just think these two individuals, Cabello, who is the biggest thief among all of them, and Tarek El Aissami in particular, are people that we should be focused on. It is not even a mystery. They do not even seem to hide it. It is just shocking to me that we have not taken it because we have done this against other people in other parts of the world, and we have named them and the world knows. There are people in the Maduro regime who are spending their weekends in Miami spending the money they are stealing from the Venezuelan people while people in Venezuela, a rich country by the way, are like rummaging through garbage in the streets every day for basic goods. It makes no sense to me.

Then you have got the right-hand man of the president of El Salvador, Jose Luis Merino. This guy is a top-notch, world-class money launderer, arms smuggler for the FARC, millions of dollars of laundering for the FARC as well as corrupt Venezuelan officials. Why is this guy not sanctioned?

Mr. MALINOWSKI. That one I will have to take back, Senator.

Senator RUBIO. Okay.

What about the FARC? You are familiar with them. This is a group that profits from cocaine smuggling, earning probably close to a billion dollars annually according to Colombian authorities and informed sources. What is our status with them vis-a-vis sanctioning them?

Mr. MALINOWSKI. Well, as far as I recall, they are on the FTO list, and they have been sanctioned over the years.

Senator RUBIO. Economically, not just named as a terrorist organization. Are we actively targeting their monies as they move them across territory and borders?

Mr. MALINOWSKI. I believe that over the years as a named foreign terrorist organization that we have done so, yes.

Senator RUBIO. And that will not be impacted by the peace deal? Has there been any discussion between the Colombian Government and ours about easing any of that as a result of this peace agreement the president of Colombia has just signed and the FARC?

Mr. MALINOWSKI. We support peace in Colombia, but I think we have been clear that in terms of our law enforcement and other equities, that that remains.

Senator RUBIO. Ms. Smith, the United States has already invested upwards of—I do not know the exact—billions of dollars, let us say, in Haiti, and most Americans understand the humanitarian nature of our response and agree with that. However, I do not think it is fair to expect the American taxpayer is going to continue to help fund elections that are overthrown because the parties are dissatisfied with the outcome. So let us have another one because we do not like who won.

So can you give us an assessment of what the current programs are in Haiti? And at this point, are they eligible to continue to receive U.S. tax dollars after what we have seen now over the last year and a half?

Ms. SMITH. Thank you, Senator. And one thing that we will do is get you a comprehensive summary of all the programs.

Again, as I mentioned earlier, the vast bulk of our assistance does not go directly to governments, so that in a country like Haiti, part of what we are trying to do is work with independent associations, civil society to do the painstaking slow work of enabling them to, again, hold governments accountable, hold up their own.

I will say to you that I think Haiti is one of the greatest development challenges we face. There is no way to cast it as otherwise. The institutions are extremely weak. Violence and crime, as you know, are on the increase. We are doing our best in some sectors to get some gains in health, food security, and so on. I think governance remains the biggest challenge. We will get you a summary of the programs.

But in terms of eligibility, I think there are a couple questions we need to think about. One, again we are very careful about cases where we provide government-to-government money. It is a tiny percentage of our budget. And I think Haiti is one where it would not make a great deal of sense.

But the second is we face the challenge as USAID and I think as the United States of sometimes not having the luxury of saying, well, this is just too hard. We are not getting any traction, so we should get out. I think we know what the consequences are in a country like Haiti if we are not present and if we disengage.

But I will also confess to you it is an uphill struggle and a constant struggle to try to get progress.

Senator RUBIO. The way I probably should have stated the question is the biggest complaint we get when we interact with them is that they want us to coordinate more of our aid through the government, even if it is not government-to-government. They want us to use their locally based organizations, the people that they pick.

And I guess my point is I am as sympathetic as anyone in the Senate about what is happening in Haiti and the plight and situation that they are facing. I also have, at this point, very low confidence, perhaps no confidence that the people they are telling us we should be working through are the right people, given the history both electorally and otherwise. We are sympathetic there. Believe me, I care deeply about what is happening there.

But what I have seen out of the political class in Haiti I should say for close to 80 years, but certainly over the last few, is unacceptable. And I will hope that as we continue to look for ways to continue to engage there, that what you are saying here is in fact the direction we are on that we continue to be on.

I will say it point blank. I have zero confidence that if the Haitian Government tells us we want you to work through this group versus that group, that there is not some deep element of corruption or even political influence at play.

I am out of time, but we also saw as well Senator Grassley's report about the lack of gains that the Red Cross made in Haiti. And we are also deeply concerned about that. Obviously, that is not necessarily taxpayer dollars. But that is the sort of challenge we face there and continue to face there because it is a place where even if you want to help, oftentimes it becomes impossible because someone needs to get paid off just to make it possible.

But I just wanted to lay out the point. This is not a forever proposition here. There has to be some progress there or I cannot justify to taxpayers, no matter how deeply moved I am about the circumstances there, that we are going to continue to pour money into a black hole where the money does not come out in a positive way.

Ms. SMITH. And if I may, Senator. I am in agreement that I cannot justify it either if we are pouring dollar after dollar without getting returns.

I think there are some places where again it is slow, but we can get traction.

But I think you also raise a very important point because on the one hand, from a development perspective, we want to strengthen government institutions and enable them to operate and not set up parallel structures. There are cases—and I think Haiti is a valid one—where if we are supporting structures or certainly being told—and we do not generally respond well to governments that tell us that you must fund this or that. That is something we make our own judgment of. But there are cases where we cannot do that, and this is one where we would be happy to continue the dialogue and work with you on it because I think we share a concern about Haiti, but also a concern about the challenges that you point out.

The CHAIRMAN. Thank you.

We thank you both for being here. I think there have been a number of good points that have come out today.

I hope that over the course of the next several months we can engage in a way to more productively deal with this. You know, corruption has such a wide range of application. In Russia, I mean, whole government systems are created that are dependent upon corruption. In China, where we think some corruption is being addressed, it is difficult to tell whether it is really addressing corruption or just weeding out rivalries so that the leadership is in a much stronger position. And then there is the petty corruption that leads to revolutions where people are, on a daily basis, harassed by law enforcement officials, having to pay to get health care. So it is wide range.

We understand in some cases we have more leverage and more ability to make change like we do in Ukraine right now where they want to move away from the Soviet model into a different era, and we are assisting them. And we have a little bit more leverage and working relationship there.

But, look, there is a lot more that we can do. It is at a huge cost in every regard to societies around the world, and we look forward to working closely with you to do more to try to overcome what we know is happening in so many places.

We thank you for your service. We have another panel that is coming up, and so we kindly dismiss you. [Laughter.]

The CHAIRMAN. I hope you have a very nice lunch and we look forward to seeing you again.

Ms. SMITH. But, Senator, just for the record, I think both of us would welcome the opportunity to work with you and members of the committee on additional things we might be able to do, some of which have been discussed this morning.

The CHAIRMAN. For what it is worth, I think there is total unanimity around this issue, Republicans and Democrats, and I do think there is a period of time when a lot of other things may not be happening because of the season that we are in. But this is one I think where we might collectively do some things that would be very positive.

Ms. SMITH. Let us seize the moment.

The CHAIRMAN. Okay, good.

Mr. MALINOWSKI. Perhaps we could discuss it over an adult beverage. [Laughter.]

The CHAIRMAN. I want to hear how it is on the inside over an adult beverage when your term is over.

Ms. SMITH. But I never got an adult beverage.

Mr. MALINOWSKI. I tell you what that is later. [Laughter.]

The CHAIRMAN. Our first witness is Mr. Carl Gershman, President of the National Endowment for Democracy. Mr. Gershman has done some important work on the nature and threat of kleptocracies and the threat of them to our national security.

Our second witness is Ms. Sarah Chayes, Senior Associate, Democracy and Rule of Law Program at the Carnegie Endowment for International Peace. I understand Ms. Chayes has firsthand experience in the challenges of corruption, having served as a special advisor to ISAF Commanders McKiernan and McChrystal on implementing anti-corruption strategies in Afghanistan.

We thank you both for sharing your knowledge and expertise with us, and if you could provide your testimony in the order I just introduced you, without objection, your entire written statement will be entered into the record. If you could summarize—I do know that Ben is going to step back in just one moment. But we thank you both for being here. And, Carl, if you would begin, we would appreciate it.

STATEMENT OF CARL GERSHMAN, PRESIDENT, THE NATIONAL ENDOWMENT FOR DEMOCRACY, WASHINGTON, D.C.

Mr. GERSHMAN. Thank you very much, Senator. I want you to know that I greatly appreciate this opportunity to testify on kleptocracy and the threat it poses to democracy and the rule of law. And I especially want to thank you for the leadership you have shown on this issue.

I want to also thank Senator Cardin for his leadership, especially on the passage of the Magnitsky Act, which in my view is the most important piece of human rights legislation in the last generation. And I applaud his efforts to globalize the application of the Magnitsky standards and mechanisms.

The scourge of corruption is generally viewed as a symptom of the larger problem of the failure of judicial, media, and other institutions of accountability in new or developing democracies.

In kleptocracies, which is the term used to designate government by thieves, corruption is the heart of the problem and the lifeblood of the system. Karen Dawisha, the author of "Putin's Kleptocracy" and one of the foremost experts on this issue, makes the observation that "in kleptocracies risk is nationalized and rewards are privatized." Participation in the spoils of kleptocracies is organized and controlled by top political elites who raid state treasuries with immunity and impunity.

Whistleblowers, investigative journalists, and others who seek to expose corrupt practices themselves become targets of law enforcement and are treated as enemies of the state. By denying space for moderate political voices that could offer possible alternatives to existing policies and leaders, kleptocracies open the way for extremists. The Azerbaijani scholar and former Reagan-Fascell fellow at NED, Altay Goyushov, observes that by repressing peaceful activists and reformers in Azerbaijan, the kleptocratic regime in Baku "argues that it is taking steps to ensure stability, but they have it exactly wrong. By eliminating moderate voices in society, Azerbaijan's leaders set the stage for an anti-Western environment that will serve as a breeding ground for extremists who pose a grave threat to both the region and to the West."

Unlike ordinary corruption, which has generally been considered a problem that corrodes developing democracies from within, kleptocracies project their corrupt practices beyond their national borders with an ever-increasing impact felt in new and established democracies alike. Kleptocracy is thus both a pillar of modern authoritarianism and a serious global threat.

Parasitic at home, kleptocratic regimes use global financial institutions to launder, invest, and protect their stolen funds, which they then use to increase their domination at home and to purchase influence abroad, all the while expanding their holdings and leverage in the West by buying extravagantly priced properties in the major global capitals. The purchase of such multi-million dollar properties, the arrangement of opaque, offshore financial instruments, and the laundering of a kleptocrat's public image cannot happen without the assistance of professional enablers—this is the issue that Senator Menendez referred to before—in the established democracies, people who are critical links in the process of securely embedding kleptocrats and their ill-gotten gains in our lawful systems.

As the journalist, Oliver Bullough, has observed "what Western enablers do is in a sense more egregious than what foreign kleptocrats do because in the West we have a genuine institutionalized rule of law while kleptocrats operate in systems where no real rules exist." These enablers both besmirch our own democracy and damage the prospect for democracy in foreign countries "even as Western governments," as Bullough says, "lecture those same countries about civil society and the rule of law."

A crucial element necessary for combating modern kleptocracy will be to bring the professional intermediaries in the West, the enablers, out of the shadows and into the sunlight.

The NED, with the support from Congress, is now devoting special attention to the issue of kleptocracy as part of an integrated strategic approach to a number of fundamental and interrelated challenges that include the crackdown on civil society, the rise of extremist movements, the failure of governance in many new democracies, the assault on democratic norms in the international system, and the weaponization of information by Russia and other autocracies.

Ending the symbiotic relationship between kleptocrats and the international financial system will be a critical dimension of our efforts. In this regard, it will be important to support activists and investigative journalists who are working within kleptocratic countries to fight state theft and to help them connect with international actors who are trying to monitor the flow of illicit capital and block its investment in the international system.

Greater cooperation among people fighting kleptocracy at different levels might also help efforts to alert publics in the democratic countries to the serious security risks they face if hostile autocracies are allowed to exploit their institutions and legal protections to aggrandize their own power. Building a new partnership between the activists fighting for the rule of law in kleptocratic countries and potential allies in the established democracies will help protect our own interests and security and advance the cause of democracy at a moment when it is in peril around the world.

Thank you, Mr. Chairman.

[Mr. Gershman's prepared statement follows:]

PREPARED STATEMENT OF CARL GERSHMAN

Mr. Chairman, thank you for the opportunity to testify before the Committee on the topic of corruption and kleptocracy. The Committee's strong voice on the corrosive impact of corruption is exceptionally important. I also want to thank you for your critical efforts to draw attention to the pervasive problem of government corruption and its implications for democratic governance and political stability.

Senator Cardin, I also would like to commend you for your leadership on the Sergei Magnitsky Act and the Global Magnitsky bill. The impact of the Sergei Magnitsky Act in spotlighting human rights abuses in Russia is visible in the tenacious—and brazen—efforts the Russian government has put into discrediting Sergei Magnitsky posthumously. A controversial film that was shown earlier this month in Washington—one that that a Washington Post editorial referred to as "agit-prop"—offers a manipulated and evidently dishonest depiction of Sergei Magnitsky. This cynical effort, and others like it, aim to remove Magnitsky's name from your pending legislation. Why? Because the Magnitsky case and the sanctions that have been imposed on key human rights abusers as a result of the act passed in his name put a sorely-needed spotlight on Russia's dangerous kleptocratic regime. The

Magnitsky Act holds such abusers to account in ways that beleaguered Russian institutions cannot, given the thorough removal of checks on power by the Putin regime.

It is important to stress at the outset that corruption is a pervasive problem in many societies and has the effect of undermining public confidence government institutions. The scourge of corruption is typically viewed as a symptom of a larger institutional problem. All countries, to one degree or another, suffer from corruption. Systems in which independent media, civil society, courts, and political opposition are weak or marginalized are particularly vulnerable because they do not possess the needed accountability and transparency to prevent corrupt practices from taking root. In kleptocracies, however, the challenge is much more acute.

In kleptocratic settings, corruption is at the heart of the problem and not chiefly a symptom of it. Karen Dawisha, the author of Putin's Kleptocracy and one of the foremost experts on this issue, makes the observation that "in kleptocracies risk is nationalized and rewards are privatized." Participation in the spoils of kleptocracies is organized and controlled by top political elites, who raid state resources with immunity and impunity.

In kleptocracies, the instruments of the state are directed to shielding and enabling the corrupt activities of dominant power holders. Corruption is the lifeblood of these systems, like the one in present day Russia, and the glue for regime survival. Therefore, in kleptocratic systems where the stakes for power are all or nothing, whistleblowers who seek to expose corrupt practices themselves routinely become targets of law enforcement; investigative journalists and oppositionists become enemies of the state; and independent businesses are brought to heel in order to preserve the kleptocratic order.

It needs to be emphasized that in the era of globalization, kleptocracy represents an exceedingly dangerous threat to democracy internationally. Corruption has generally been considered a problem that corrodes developing democracies from within. Well-resourced kleptocracies differ in that they project their sophisticated corrupt practices beyond national borders with an ever-increasing impact felt in new and established democracies alike. Kleptocracy has emerged a serious global threat. Parasitic at home, abroad kleptocratic regimes by their nature seek to exploit the vulnerabilities in the institutions of individual democratic states, as well as regional and global rules-based institutions. They use global financial institutions to invest and protect their money, and with their stolen resources, they buy influence in the democracies and neutralize political opposition. Kleptocracy has become a crucial pillar of the international resurgence of authoritarian countries.

For these reasons, and with support from the Congress, the National Endowment for Democracy is devoting special attention to the issue of kleptocracy as part of a dedicated, strategic response to a number of fundamental and inter-related challenges that characterize different aspects of the present crisis of democracy.

In addition to kleptocracy, NED will be focusing strategic attention on five key problems: the systematic assault by authoritarian regimes on international democratic norms and values; the failure of transition and effective governance in many countries where autocrats have fallen; the rise of Islamist and other forms of religious and sectarian extremism; the closing of civic space in scores of countries; and an information offensive by Russia and other authoritarian regimes that is influencing opinion and undermining the integrity of the information space in many regions.

While aspects of these problems have long been common to systems of absolute power, together they represent a more formidable and integrated threat to democracy than anything the world has experienced since the end of the Cold War. NED will continue to fund programs that support democracy efforts in specific countries, but it is also fashioning a new approach that consists of effective transnational responses to key strategic challenges. In doing so, it will be able to build on its record over more than three decades of addressing critical challenges to democracy, and to leverage the experience and expertise of its core institutes and many dedicated partners around the world.

COMBATING MODERN KLEPTOCRACY

Returning to the principal subject of today's hearing, I would like to reemphasize the serious threat posed by modern kleptocracy.

Until now, NED has supported anti-corruption, transparency, and accountability projects, but has not focused on the transnational impact and phenomenon of modern kleptocracies and their negative impact on democratic, norms, values, and institutions in democratic and democratizing countries.

I will stress several key points relating to the challenge posed by kleptocracy:

Kleptocracy is a global threat. The taking of money out of corrupt countries by kleptocrats is a long-standing practice—think of Mobutu Sese Seko's Zaire and Ferdinand Marcos' Philippines—but in the present hyper-globalized era the scale and sophistication of this activity presents new and serious challenges to democracy. In this sense, and as the Panama Papers so vividly reveal, modern kleptocracy thrives by crossing borders, in the process projecting a wider, corrosive threat to democracy and its institutions.

Kleptocracy is a key pillar of the global authoritarian resurgence that is visible in so many critical spheres. This includes in regional and international organizations, activities such as election monitoring and the autocrats' treatment of civil society, as well as the projection of propaganda through lavishly funded international media enterprises, such as the Russian government's RT. Simply put, these regimes are reshaping the rules of the game.

The challenge presented by regimes in Moscow, Beijing, and elsewhere is being taken to an entirely new level by virtue of their projection of illiberal values and standards beyond their own national borders. Just a decade ago, few political observers could even have imagined such a development. It's especially troubling that this growth in authoritarian ambition is taking place at a time when malaise seems to grip the world's leading democracies.

Kleptocracy Subverts Democracy. Kleptocrats exploit the benefits of globalization to enrich themselves, hollow out their own countries' institutions, and subvert the democracies. Given these particular features, kleptocracy should be understood as an especially acute subset of corrupt systems. The issue of kleptocracy is an important one for activists who are working for democracy in countries ruled by hybrid and autocratic governments. Such activists are on the frontlines in the struggle against resurgent authoritarianism where regimes are tightening political controls and closing civic space. The activists who took to the Maidan in Ukraine sought to extract their country from the kleptocratic grip of former President Viktor Yanukovych.

Deeply entrenched corruption has been an extraordinary challenge since Ukraine achieved its independence a quarter century ago. But in the four years that he was in power, Yanukovych took the country's corruption to new heights, enabling the theft of a vast amount of Ukraine's public wealth. As the analyst Anders Aslund notes, nearly $40 billion was estimated to have been stolen from the state while Yanukovych was in power. This massive corruption funneled wealth primarily to the president, his relatives, and a limited circle of businessmen around the president. This systematic corruption has ravaged Ukraine and has been central to its population's determination to chart a more democratically accountable course.

As journalist Oliver Bullough observes: "In 1991, Ukraine's GDP was about two-thirds of Poland's GDP; now it is less than one quarter." He notes that state corruption on such a scale has ruined Ukraine, "dooming a generation of Ukrainians to poor education, unsafe streets and blighted careers." The responsibility for such massive theft does not lie with unscrupulous Ukrainians alone, however. There would not be corruption on such a vast and sophisticated scale without offshore centers like Panama. "If you steal money, you need somewhere to launder it; otherwise it is useless." This raises the important issue of Western enablers, a subject which I will return to shortly.

Azerbaijan has descended into an ever more repressive and kleptocratic form of governance. Journalists who seek to report on the extraordinary corruption of the country's ruling elite end up in jail, or worse. Courageous Khadija Ismailiyova, who produced detailed investigative reporting linking the family of Azerbaijani President Ilham Aliyev to massive corrupt enterprises, was sent to prison on patently trumped up charges. She was released last month. As Gerald Knaus points out in a July 2015 Journal of Democracy issue titled "Europe and Azerbaijan: The End of Shame," Azerbaijan's kleptocracy has a profound and corrosive effect within but also beyond the country's borders. Knaus explains in painful detail the ways in which the authorities in Azerbaijan "captured" the Council of Europe and in the process managed to neuter its human rights work.

In Angola, as journalists such as Rafael Marques de Morais have observed, the country's political elite has taken control of virtually all of the country's public wealth. Here, too, the Angolan kleptocrats do not simply deprive their own country of critically needed resources for improving health, education, and infrastructure, but use this wealth beyond national borders to acquire an influential hand in media and financial institutions inside EU member state Portugal. Russia's kleptocracy has managed similar feats in Latvia, also an EU member state.

The fact that these authoritarian regimes are also kleptocratic makes the challenge facing democracy activists in such countries even more difficult. This is because the kleptocrats have been able to establish an objective alliance with banks and other institutions that make up the global financial system. These institutions readily receive the stolen funds after they have been laundered through various offshore structures. With these assets safely invested and protected within the global system, the kleptocrats can then use the stolen funds to increase their domination at home and to purchase influence abroad, all the while expanding their holdings and leverage in the West and buying extravagantly priced properties in London, New York, Miami, and other global capitals.

The problem of Western enablers. The purchase of multimillion dollar properties, the arrangement of opaque offshore financial instruments, and the laundering of a kleptocrat's public image, do not happen by accident or on its own. Professional intermediaries in the established democracies are critical links for venal kleptocrats who seek to move ill-gotten gains from authoritarian systems into the democracies, where they can enjoy the rule of law. As journalist Bullough observes, "only with the help of Western enablers can a foreign kleptocrat transform the ownership of a questionable fortune, earned in an unstable country where jail is often one court decision away, into a respected philanthropist" who can be photographed alongside celebrated international figures and media stars.

Anne Applebaum has noted the irony that while the rule of law prevails in Britain, "over the past couple of decades, London's accountants and lawyers have helped launder billions of dollars of stolen money through the British Virgin Islands, among other British overseas territories." Their complicity in kleptocracy has corroded the legal integrity of the British system. As Bullough notes, "what Western enablers do is in a sense more egregious than what foreign kleptocrats do, because in the West we have a genuine, institutionalized rule of law, while kleptocrats operate in systems where no real rules exist. The result is that Western enablers effectively undermine democracy in foreign countries, even as Western governments lecture those same countries about civil society and the rule of law." A crucial element necessary for combating modern kleptocracy will be bringing the professional intermediaries in the West—the enablers—out of the shadows and into the sunlight.

Kleptocracy is an engine for extremism. Kleptocratic governments by their nature extinguish or prevent the emergence of institutions that can hold them accountable, leading to governance arrangements that feature unchecked power and impunity. This is the modus operandi of "rule by thieves." Critically, kleptocratic regimes deny space for moderate political voices that could offer possible alternatives to existing policies and leaders. In the kleptocracies of Eurasia and the Middle East, for instance, this kind of harsh political marginalization, where virtually all moderate voices are targeted, opens the way for extremists. Azerbaijani scholar Altay Goyushov observes that by repressing peaceful activists and reformers in Azerbaijan, the kleptocratic regime in Baku "argues that it is taking steps to ensure stability. They have this exactly wrong. By eliminating moderate voices in society, Azerbaijan's leaders set the stage for anti-Western environment that will serve as a breeding ground for extremists, who pose a grave security threat to both the region and the West."

RESPONDING TO THE CHALLENGE

Because kleptocracy is a global challenge it requires a response that takes the transnational nature of this problem into account. To this end, NED is at the beginning stages of an effort to analyze the scope and key elements of this problem, while deepening linkages among existing country-level anti-kleptocracy initiatives and those working at the regional or international level. We will look to expand and strengthen existing anti-corruption efforts that address key components of kleptocratic systems and support efforts by civil society and journalists to challenge regimes, leaders and institutions that are perpetuating kleptocracy.

Ending the symbiotic relationship between kleptocrats and the international financial system will be a critical dimension of our efforts. In this regard, it will be important to support activists and investigative journalists who are working within kleptocratic countries to fight state theft and to help them connect with international actors who are trying to monitor the flow of illicit capital and block its investment in the international financial system. We must identify how grassroots activists and such international actors can find more effective ways of working with and supporting each other. Through such cooperation, we hope that the activists will find new allies and outlets for their investigative reports, while the international actors will gain useful contact with indigenous groups whose knowledge of the way funds are stolen might contribute to the development of laws and strategies to block the receipt of these funds by the global banking system.

Greater cooperation among people fighting kleptocracy at different levels might also help efforts to alert the publics in democratic countries to the serious security risks they face by allowing hostile autocracies to exploit their institutions and legal protections to aggrandize their own power. Just as it is urgently important to end the corrupting collaboration between the kleptocrats and their enablers, it is equally important to build a new partnership between the activists fighting for the rule of law in kleptocratic countries and potential allies in the established democracies who are committed to the defense of democratic values. Building such a partnership will help protect our own interests and security and advance the cause of democracy at a moment when it is in peril around the world.

Thank you, again, for the opportunity to contribute this testimony.

The CHAIRMAN. Thank you.

Ms. Chayes?

STATEMENT OF SARAH CHAYES, SENIOR ASSOCIATE, DEMOCRACY AND RULE OF LAW PROGRAM, CARNEGIE ENDOWMENT FOR INTERNATIONAL PEACE, WASHINGTON, D.C.

Ms. CHAYES. Thank you very much, Chairman Corker. It is a delight to see you again. Ranking Member Cardin, thank you both for holding this hearing and for inviting me to participate.

I think the proceedings so far have done a pretty good job illustrating the scope of the problem. I would just like to dwell for a second on some of the immaterial aspects that are at least as important as the financial aspects.

When a cop shakes you down at the side of the road, he does not do it politely. There is a kind of scalding humiliation that is part of this whole problem, the injustice that I think we have talked about, the betrayal, when it is the very government officials you would turn to for help who are actually doing the abuses.

The second point—and I think this was raised by Carl in the word "kleptocracy"—we are not talking about just a collection of nasty behaviors on the part of a certain number of officials. This is the actually the operating system of sophisticated networks that are successful at doing what they are setting out to do, which is maximizing returns for network members. Right? They are sophisticated and successful and structured. If anything, they are more like an integrated criminal organization than they are like a weak or fragile government. And by that, I mean they are integrating across into the private sector, as well as the public sector, into the criminal sector, as we have just been hearing. And they are vertically integrated. That cop shaking down the person on the street is sending a part of the money upwards. So all of these impacts on government function are deliberate. That means both the bending of certain government functions to serve these purposes and also the hollowing out. The ghost soldiers or ghost health workers are in fact deliberate.

I would say about 62 countries in the world fall into this category, and they are listed in my written testimony.

How does this relate to security? I think, Mr. Cardin, you set that out just as well as I could, so I am going to skip over except to emphasize a little bit the connection to violent extremism. It is not just that somebody who might be against violent extremism will not report to the police. It is that when you are abused in this way, it becomes a really persuasive argument for, for example, the head of what is now called Boko Haram. Residents of Maiduguri told me—here is what they were saying. They were saying that if only our government followed God's law, this kind of thing would not be happening. That is the argument.

So let us stop a minute. That means that a lot of U.S. counterterrorism support, when it has the effect of reinforcing such a government, is in fact counterproductive. It is a really, I think, critical consideration here.

So what are we doing about it? I think we heard a lot to that effect earlier. And it is true that more than at any other time in the decade I have been working on this hard, we are doing something. But I have to say as critical as they are or the very critical transparency initiatives that are the focus of most of the effort and which we heard Mr. Malinowski discuss—I just do not think they are going to make much of a dent, certainly not alone. And I will get into sort of why.

But secondly, frankly this issue is still offloaded onto under-resourced and under-appreciated specialists in the bureaucracies we have been talking about. It is a subset of INL at the State Department. It is seen as not a great career choice at State. I mean, I have just been talking to folks in the last couple days. At USAID, which spends billions, as we have been discussing, in corrupt environments, twice as many officers are assigned to the important issue of LGBT rights as are assigned to corruption. And—this is probably the most important—the effect of the anti-corruption efforts or demarches is overshadowed by the gigantic military and other types of assistance projects that are delivered. This mismatch is so great that from the perspective of a corrupt leader, the U.S. is not even contradictory. It is clear. It is okay with corruption. The lip service really is just a sop to you.

And so I think, again, Senator Corker, you showed the way. The question is not so much what is the anti-corruption programming. It is how are the flagship efforts like Power Africa addressing the problem.

What can you do? I would actually suggest that rather than the reporting requirements about what is a government doing to fight corruption, which will often be a charade, you should be requiring that for every budget request for a military and civilian program greater than a certain level there be a political economy analysis that actually susses out what is the structure and functioning of the corrupt system in that country and how is that programming going to mitigate those possibilities.

I think I have just got two other things.

You should direct State to develop these analyses and put them into the read-aheads on every DC and PC on the 62 countries I am talking about. Direct both of these agencies to increase billets and frankly move some of—I know this is not for you in this committee, but work to move some of the DOD counterterrorism funding across to deal with some of these issues. Training, finally, is really critical. It should be mandatory in both of these agencies that officers do corruption analysis training.

Thank you very much.

[Ms. Chayes's prepared statement follows.]

Prepared Statement of Sarah Chayes

I'd like to thank Chairman Corker for holding this important hearing. Just calling it has already had the salutary impact of challenging officials in the foreign policy and assistance communities to think through the implications of corruption for their operations. And my thanks also to Ranking Member Cardin for extending this invitation for me to testify today.

There is a growing recognition of the impact of corruption on the U.S. national interest. Signs of the rising awareness can be found in recent official statements. "From the Arab Spring to Latin America," wrote U.S. Secretary of State John Kerry in May, "political turbulence has made clear that governments are unwise to shrug off their citizens' growing concerns about corruption. ... It is long past time for the international community to treat corruption with the seriousness and attention it deserves." [1]

And yet, given the consequences of the type of sophisticated and systemic corruption that has taken widespread hold in the past quarter-century, especially its impact on global stability and the legitimacy of governments—and therefore on the U.S. national interest—the policy approaches to the problem remain disproportionately weak.

The issue of corruption should be central to foreign and international trade policy development and should inform the way U.S. assistance—military as well as civilian—is shaped. Members of Congress can provide important guidance to the executive branch to help make that happen.

THE SCOPE OF GLOBAL CORRUPTION

Given the mesmerizing capacity of numbers to focus our imaginations these big-data days, it is tempting to seek a dollar figure to quantify the scale of corruption worldwide. By its nature, of course, that is a fraught proposition, given the incentives for the corrupt to conceal their deeds and the facilities the current globalized economy offers them for doing so.

The non-profit organization Global Financial Integrity, for example, uses strict methodologies to derive an estimate as to the quantity of money illicitly departing developing countries annually.[2] That number, however, leaves out cash transfers, whereas millions certainly[3] and doubtless billions of physical dollars are shipped around by the criminal and the corrupt each year. It also mixes the proceeds of corruption with the proceeds of other sorts of criminality in its reckoning. And it misses all corruptly obtained money that is spent within the countries where it was looted.[4]

But even if it were possible to arrive at a fair estimate of the sum siphoned into the pockets of the corrupt each year, that would not constitute an adequate measure of the scope of the problem. At least as important as the monetary losses corruption inflicts on countries and their populations is the damage of a less material order.

When a policeman or a doctor or a registrar of deeds demands a pay-off, he or she doesn't do it politely. The shakedown is typically accompanied by arrogant contempt. The victims—like that young Tunisian who lit himself on fire in 2011, setting off the Arab Spring revolutions—suffer scalding humiliation alongside the theft of their scarce resources.

The injustice of the way the whole system functions compounds the injury. It's not as though everyone is poor side-by-side. When people have to walk past huge mansions with strings of electric lights burning day and night while the power is cut off to their part of town, or when they keep being forced to jump aside when a swish SUV splashes past them on a pitted street, and when they know the money to buy these things has been skimmed off of public works or development contracts—or has been extorted from people like them—the sense of personal injury

---

[1] John Kerry, "Time to Treat Corruption With the Seriousness It Deserves," U.S. Department of State, May 12, 2016, accessed June 28, 2016 at http://www.state.gov/secretary/remarks/2016/05/257175.htm. *See also* his remarks delivered at "Against Corruption," a summit hosted by British Prime Minister David Cameron on May 12, 2016, accessed June 28, 2016 at http://www.state.gov/secretary/remarks/2016/05/257130.htm

[2] Global Financial Integrity (GFI), "Data by Country," accessed June 27, 2016 at http://www.gfintegrity.org/issues/data-by-country/.

[3] According to reporting by the Wall Street Journal in 2010, as much as $10 million per day was leaving Afghanistanat that time, much but hardly all of it declared. Matthew Rosenberg, "Corruption Suspected in Airlift of Billions in Cash from Kabul," Wall Street Journal June 25, 2010. A U.S. intelligence professional told me that millions of dollars in cash had been flown out of Nigeria in the wake of the March 2015 election of Muhammadu Buhari as president.

[4] *See* GFI's methodological note here: http://www.gfintegrity.org/issues/illicit-financial-flows-analytical-methodologies-utilized-global-financial-integrity/

grows. And with the expanding availability of information through the electronic media, such juxtapositions are on increasing display.

Especially galling to many victims of corruption is that the very officials to whom they might turn to report the abuses are the primary abusers themselves. As an indignant young Afghan man put it to me in 2009, referring to the police, "They're supposed to be defending the law, and they're the ones breaking it!"

Far from representing an accepted "part of the culture," in other words, as so many Westerners surmise, corruption is experienced as a bitter betrayal by people I have interviewed in nearly a dozen countries on three continents, corroding their respect for their public institutions. They see their governments as a hostile force—against which, of course, there is no recourse. They and other victims are left either to suffer or rebel.

All too frequently, and contrary to conventional wisdom, corrupt practices can't be summed up as the venal behavior of a certain number of individuals. They represent a sophisticated set of operating procedures employed by a successful, if sometimes loosely structured or contentious, network. This is a final point to bear in mind when considering the "scope" of the problem. The street-level foot soldiers in these corruption syndicates—the cops or the clerks or the customs officials who shake down ordinary people—are passing part of their take up the line, just like rank-and-file members of the Mafia.

At the top, the syndicates typically bend parts of the government apparatus to serve their purposes, be it the tax authority, the justice sector, the legislature, or the ministry of energy and industry. Other agencies may pose a threat, or command a fat budget that can be pillaged. Such was the fate of the Iraqi and Nigerian militaries, both of which collapsed when challenged in 2014. Their platoons were filled with ghost soldiers who existed on paper only, their officers collecting their pay. Officers had been selling materiel, leaving those troops who did take the field disarmed before the enemy.[5]

Another way these networks pursue their self-enrichment goals is to integrate across to the private sector. The principal companies in industries most likely to benefit from government contracting or concessions, such as construction or mining or energy, are owned by the president's daughter or son-in-law or by retired generals. Network members dominate regulated sectors, such as telecoms and banking. In Azerbaijan, for example, the family of President Ilham Aliyev owns no fewer than eleven banks.[6]

The structured nature of so many of these systems poses an added problem of scope for policymakers. It means that remedies aimed at individual corrupt actors and their facilitators are important but insufficient. The challenge is one of policy alignment, for at least minimal consistency across the disparate agencies of the U.S. government, so as to send a legible message to corrupt networks and truly affect their incentive structures.

Based on research I have been conducting over the past five years, I estimate the number of countries that fall into this category of widespread and systemic corruption at just over 60.[7]

---

[5] *See,* for example, David Kirkpatrick, "Graft Hobbles Iraq's Military in Fighting ISIS," New York Times November 23, 2014, or Aryn Baker, "Nigeria's Military Quails When Faced with Boko Haram," Time Magazine, February 10, 2015.

[6] Organized Crime and Corruption Reporting Project, "Azerbaijani First Family Big on Banking" June 11, 2015, accessed June 28, 2016 at https://www.occrp.org/en/corruptistan/azerbaijan/2015/06/11/azerbaijani-first-family-big-on-banking.html, For a full discussion of the way kleptocratic elites structure their networks, see Sarah Chayes, "The Structure of Corruption: A Systemic Analysis," Carnegie Endowment for International Peace, expected July 1, 2016.

[7] The countries are: Afghanistan, Algeria, Angola, Armenia, Azerbaijan, Bahrain, Bangladesh, Brazil, Bulgaria, Burkina Faso, Burundi, Cameroon, Chad, China, Colombia, Cote d'Ivoire, Egypt, Equatorial Guinea, Eritrea, Ethiopia, Guatemala Guinea, Guinea-Bissau, Guyana, Honduras, Iceland, India, Indonesia, Kazakhstan, Kenya, Kyrgyzstan, Lebanon, Libya, Mali, Mexico, Moldova, Morocco, Nepal, Niger, Nigeria, Pakistan, Paraguay, Philippines, Romania, Sierra Leone, Slovenia, Somalia, South Africa, South Sudan, Sudan, Syria, Tajikistan, Thailand, Tunisia, Turkey, Turkmenistan, Uganda, Ukraine, Uzbekistan, Venezuela, Yemen, and Zimbabwe. This list was derived by Carnegie Junior Fellow Julu Katticaran by aggregating the following indices: The African Development Bank Country Policy and Institutional Assessments, Afrobarometer, Asian Development Bank Country Policy and Institutional Assessments, European Bank for Reconstruction and Development Transition Report, Economist Intelligence Unit Riskwire and Democracy Index, Freedom House, Global Integrity Index, Gallup World Poll, International Budget Project Open Budget Index, Latinobarometro Sustainability Index, Political Economic Risk Consultancy Corruption in Asia Survey, Political Risk Services International Country Risk Guide, Transparency International Corruption Perceptions Index and Global Cor-

Continued

HOW CORRUPTION IMPACTS NATIONAL AND INTERNATIONAL SECURITY

It's hard to miss the rising level of indignation at the kind of systemic and often ostentatious corruption described above. In just the past year, popular protests have broken out in Azerbaijan, Brazil, Guatemala, Honduras, Iraq, Lebanon, Malaysia, Moldova, and Venezuela. Two chiefs of state have fallen.

But not all the victims have been able to express their frustration in such relatively civil ways. The revolutions of the Arab Spring and Ukraine represent, at least in part, more determined variations on such anti-corruption protests. In every country that erupted in 2011, demonstrators denounced the corruption of detested ruling cliques, and demanded legal accounting for corrupt officials and a return of looted assets.

Those revolutions have degenerated into some of the chief security challenges Washington is currently confronting: a lingering East-West stand-off on the redrawn Ukrainian frontier, slaughter in Syria, the implosion of Libya, Yemen and part of Iraq, and an expanding insurgency in Egypt.

For, corruption fuels the scourge of terrorism too: it gives credence to the arguments of militant religious extremists such as the self-proclaimed Islamic State, and has helped them gain recruits or submissiveness from Afghanistan and Iraq to Pakistan, Central Asia, the Sahel, and West Africa. The pitch is a simple one, rooted in the manifest moral deviance of the corrupt: "They were saying the truth about the violations committed by government agencies," residents of Maiduguri, Nigeria told me during an outdoor conversation on November 21, 2015, explaining the early preaching of the extremist group Boko Haram. "They said, if our constitution were based on the Islamic system, all these things wouldn't be happening; it would be a just and fair society."

It may seem a spurious argument, especially in light of the behavior of extremist organizations when they gain power (including the government of Iran). But it can be awfully persuasive to a young Nigerian man whose sister has just been fondled by a professor as the cost of matriculation. Indeed, a glance at Western history, including our own, indicates that militant puritanical religion is a frequent reaction to abusively corrupt governance.[8]

The anger is not just directed against host-country governments, either. When the United States is seen as intimately associated with the corrupt practices, victims not unreasonably assume our country explicitly approves them. "The Afghan government is your face," a member of my manufacturing cooperative in downtown Kandahar, Afghanistan told me one day. "If it's pretty or it's ugly, it's your face."

In light of this reality, counterterrorism partnerships that reinforce abusively corrupt governments may be doing more harm than good. They may lead to the radicalization of a dozen people for every one that is killed, and excite anger against the U.S. patron as well as the venal local client.

Other security challenges that are inflamed by corruption include chronic outbreaks of violence due to rivalry among competing kleptocratic networks (as in Somalia or the Democratic Republic of Congo, for example)[9] and the reinforcement of transnational organized crime structures through their interpenetration with corrupt governments in their home bases (as in Central America or the Balkans). It would not be unreasonable to ascribe even some of the adventurism of China and Russia to corruption, and an effort to distract a restive population from its grievances via an appeal to nationalist feeling.

THE EFFECTIVENESS OF CURRENT ANTI-CORRUPTION EFFORTS

There is no question that corruption has attracted measurably increased policy attention over the past year, not just in words but in deed. Some 30 investigators have been added to the U.S. Department of Justice's anti-kleptocracy unit; the State Department's regional bureaus now feature an anti-corruption assignment; and the United States is participating in several multinational law enforcement initiatives aimed at information sharing and asset recovery.

Still, given the dimensions of the problem, the approaches adopted to date have been sadly inadequate.

---

ruption Barometer Survey, U.S. State Department Trafficking in People report, World Justice Project Rule of Law Index, plus my own qualitative corroboration as to degree of structure.

[8] For a complete discussion of how puritanical religion is often a reaction to severe corruption, *see* Sarah Chayes, Thieves of State: Why Corruption Threatens Global Security (New York: W.W. Norton, 2015).

[9] *See* Alex de Waal, The Real Politics of the Horn of Africa: Money, Politics, and the Business of Power (New York: Polity, 2015). Note de Waal uses the terminology of the marketplace, rather than corruption, but the his description applies.

Corruption, first of all, is typically viewed as a functional specialization, and a poorly rewarded one at that. It is subcontracted to often marginal units within the State Department or USAID: the Bureau of International Narcotics and Law Enforcement Affairs, for example, where it counts, presumably, as a subset of law enforcement. According to two young officials reflecting on the atmosphere within the State Department over the past several months, the mention of corruption is met with "rolled eyes," in one bureau; elsewhere interest in the topic is seen as a career-killer.

At USAID, an organization whose business model entails investing millions of dollars per year into severely corrupt environments, a comparison between the number of personnel assigned to LGBT rights, clearly a vital issue touching fundamental human dignity, and the number of people assigned to corruption might be instructive.

Where steps are being taken, moreover, they are scattershot. Decisions to pursue kleptocracy investigations are made by front-line investigators, on the sole basis of the quality of evidence that has come to hand, not any deliberate strategy. The focus on beneficial ownership or transparency initiatives carries with it the implication that corruption is the work of disconnected individuals, who can be taken on individually. Transparency becomes an end in itself, when too often it fails to result in ultimate accountability. Support to civil society groups is provided in blissful isolation from the countervailing incentives that other aspects of U.S. engagement may be providing to a corrupt leadership. Sometimes the contradiction puts beleaguered activists or reformist government officials in impossible, even life-threatening, situations.

Indeed, it is this disconnect that likely precludes current U.S. anti-corruption programming from having any noticeable impact. When Washington is providing millions of dollars in military and development assistance, or when the CIA station chief is handing over a similar sum per month to a corrupt leader in private meetings, as has been the case in Afghanistan,[10] a few hundred thousand dollars spent on capacity building for the inspector general of police, for example, or to support a civic group agitating for budget transparency, is almost laughable. Indeed, viewed from the perspective of the corrupt leader, U.S. policy is hardly even contradictory; it's clear: the United States approves of his venal practices, and the occasional public scolding or paltry anti-corruption programming must surely just be designed to check a box or mollify Congress, rather than to convey any meaningful message as to U.S. policy.

It is in this light that the U.S. Congress should frame its questions to the military and civilian assistance communities. It is not so important to ask what is being spent on what programs designed to curb corruption, but rather what steps are being taken to shape flagship projects, such as Power Africa, or our military partnership with Ethiopia, in such a way that their implementation and outcomes don't inadvertently benefit the kleptocratic network.

RECOMMENDATIONS

The Foreign Relations Committee can push Congress to help remedy some of these deficiencies in approach by taking the following steps.

- ♦ For every assistance package (USAID, INL, and State Department-overseen military programming) of significant size, require that a systemic political economy analysis, depicting the structure of corrupt networks, the main revenue streams they capture, and their key external enablers and facilitators be completed and submitted to Congress alongside the funding request.[11]
- ♦ Require that such a request include a strategy for mitigating any reinforcement the programming might provide to the corrupt governing system.
- ♦ Require that budgets for projects that, due to some other security or diplomatic imperative, are knowingly launched in severely corrupt environments devote a greater than normal proportion of the funds to monitoring and evaluation; require that the RFP or project design include provisions for citizens' oversight of project delivery, and suspension or cancellation where misuse of funds is discovered. Improvement of governance should be considered as an equally important goal of such projects as their stated objectives.
- ♦ Redirect some appropriations away from the already well-resourced U.S. Department of Defense counterterrorism or countering-violent-extremism program-

---

[10] Matthew Rosenberg, "With Bags of Cash, CIA Seeks Influence in Afghanistan," New York Times, April 28, 2013.

[11] For a template for such an analysis, see Chayes "Structure."

ming toward civilian-led activities that can help curb partner governments' corruption and dissociate the United States from it.

♦ Direct the U.S. Department of State and USAID to increase the number of billets, including intelligence billets, for personnel deeply versed in corruption and its implications for the broad range of programming and diplomatic relations. (And direct USAID to spend its allocated anti-corruption budget to this effect, instead of passing it along to State.)

♦ Direct the U.S. Department of State to develop mandatory training on the implications of corruption, its structure and functioning, and ways in which diplomatic relations, trade promotion, and civilian and military assistance interact with it, for all political, economy, and political-military officers.

There are a variety of other actions Congress could take that lie outside the purview of this Committee. I would be happy to elaborate as appropriate.

Please accept my gratitude for the opportunity to contribute to this deliberation.

The CHAIRMAN. Thank you very much. Thank you both for that testimony.

Senator Cardin?

Senator CARDIN. I also want to join the chairman in thanking you for the testimony. And I agree with much of what both of you have stated.

Ms. Chayes, in regards to your recommendations on political economy analysis, I think that would be very helpful, and we will certainly take a look at that particular proposal.

Let me ask both of you. There are countries that have serious corruption problems that are our strategic partners in the war against terror. We provide foreign military assistance to these countries. How would you urge us to use that relationship where we are providing military assistance to countries that have serious corruption issues? How should we deal with that?

Mr. GERSHMAN. Senator Cardin, first of all, while you were out——

Senator CARDIN. I heard you. Thank you very much for your compliment.

Mr. GERSHMAN. Yes. And I want you to know how deeply we feel that because of the importance of the Magnitsky Act and everything you have done on that.

My own feeling is that the research that has been done on corruption and dealing with the problem of corruption underlines the fact that building an enlightened citizenry with collective action capacity is one of these most important things that can be done in fighting corruption and kleptocracy. And this can be done through strengthening civil society, investigative journalists, and so forth. And where we have this kind of a strategic relationship, I think it gives the United States greater leverage in the relationship to keep the space open for civil society to develop and for investigative journalists to report. Obviously, we can use our own leverage on those governments to try to influence their behavior, but I think the most important thing we can do is to protect and open the way for the society in those countries to emphasize normative values, which is the most effective way ultimately to combat corruption.

Ms. CHAYES. On the political economy analysis, I can help offline with what that might look like, what the components might be.

I agree that civil society is really important, but I sometimes feel like we are offloading all of the responsibility onto often beleaguered and very fragile civil society organizations. I mean, today I just had a conversation with somebody working in the Pol-Mil Bureau in State, and this person said literally she raises the word corruption," and people roll their eyes. So it is not yet plugged into the mainstream planning on this most critical issue.

We have watched billions of dollars go into deliberately disabled militaries in Iraq, in Afghanistan, et cetera. I think, number one, Pol-Mil needs to go through some of this training. And the same goes for the Defense Department in CT.

Number two, in countries like this, our military assistance should have as large a governance component as it does a shooting component. In other words, part of the objective needs to be to teach people in these militaries that how they treat their populations is as important in dealing with terrorism as how well they shoot terrorists.

Senator CARDIN. Thank you.

Mr. Gershman, I did hear your compliment, and thank you very much for that.

I want both of you to respond to the two largest countries of concern, and that is Russia and China. We spent a lot of time in Russia. The Magnitsky bill—we are looking at making that global. It has passed the Senate but it has also passed the House committee, and we are working on that. The amount of corruption in both of those countries is alarming. What more can the United States do to advance good governance and anti-corruption issues in Russia and in China?

Mr. GERSHMAN. Senator Cardin, that is obviously a very tough question. These are two very, very difficult countries.

I note—and I did not really talk about China even in my written testimony, but in the Panama Papers, it reveals that the family members of eight senior Chinese communist officials own companies abroad from China. So despite their anti-corruption campaign, which is really internal politics, the abuse is enormous.

And with Russia, it is such an unpredictable and in my view unstable situation. And I think there is a tendency on the part of people here to give up on internal forces in Russia, to say that they have passed these laws and you cannot do anything. I mean, they have declared us to be undesirable. But that has not stopped us, and we are going forward. And there are people in Russia who have enormous courage and are continuing, and you never know what is going to happen. I believe that and I was told by the U.S. Ambassador that Putin watches videos of Qaddafi. He feels very, very insecure. So these are unpredictable circumstances, and we cannot abandon the internal forces, weak as they are right now, who offer an alternative to this kind of system.

And I would say the same goes for China. The Xi regime itself is feeling deeply insecure about its own power. There were those incidents in March, as you may remember, where on a regime website an open letter appeared calling upon Xi to resign.

So these are unstable situations. And in those types of situations, I do not think we should give up on the support for people inside the system who want to have a system based upon universal values, which is what they call what they want. They believe in universal values. And so I think we have to defend those universal values with much greater vigor than we have.

Senator CARDIN. So, Ms. Chayes, I want you to respond, if you could. It is interesting. In Russia, they have done everything they can to shut down civil societies. In China, it is a challenge for civil societies. We have little direct leverage from the point of view of our resources. We do have leverage in our relationship with China. Any suggestions?

Ms. CHAYES. So I would look a little bit at the different complexions of these two countries. I would actually take Xi at his word and say, look, we recognize this priority that you have given to anti-corruption. Here is what some of the implications of that would be. And that means not just corruption inside China. It also means who is China dealing with and how elsewhere in the world, in particular in Africa and in Central Asia. So that is sort of where I would go with that, and that is a diplomatic challenge. But it means this becomes one of the major issues for bilaterals with China.

With Russia, I think that it is important to start looking—again, these networks, integrated transnational networks. So let us take the banking system in Moldova, which is a pretty important, if small, ally of ours. Well, the banking system in Moldova is an external network member of Russian organized kleptocratic networks. Right? So let us look at how—other ways. I mean, again, Magnitsky is fantastic. But what are some of the other ways that we can make that type of activity more costly and painful?

Senator CARDIN. Thank you both.

Mr. Chairman, I would ask unanimous consent that the statement from the Department of Justice, which I understand we recently received, be made part of our record.

The CHAIRMAN. Without objection.

[The prepared statement of Department of Justice is located in the Additional Material Submitted for the Record section at the end of this publication.]

The CHAIRMAN. You made a comment about Boko Haram. It was an anecdotal statement, I know, by someone in Nigeria I assume. So we do help other governments with anti-terrorism and we are viewed as assisting governments then that are corrupt, and in some ways it creates adverse feelings towards our own country.

Again, I know you do not know every opinion in the world that exists, but here we are talking about China. We are talking about Russia. We could talk about Venezuela. We could talk about North Korea. We could talk about a lot of countries.

Generally speaking, how do you think people outside of our own country view the United States as it relates to these types of issues?

Ms. CHAYES. I have spent a lot of time on the ground, and I have to say we are not viewed very well. That is really back to what I was saying about the disproportion between the type of support that is provided highly to kleptocratic governments and then the kind of anti-corruption maybe lip service that is paid. You know, when you have got the United States Government—and we have communicated about this issue in the past. When the United States Government is providing suitcases or bags of cash in private meetings to a highly corrupt president, the people of that country quite naturally say, oh, you want the corruption. You are in favor of the corruption.

The CHAIRMAN. And that public official talks about it publicly.

Ms. CHAYES. Correct, correct. That was an egregious example, but I think it is happening all around the world.

And so I think at the moment United States credibility is extremely weak on these issues. Extremely weak, to the point that, as I said before, I think some of the efforts that we are doing are so flimsy in comparison to the apparent support provided to corrupt governments that it looks like plausible deniability in a way. It looks, as I say, like a sop to you Members of Congress. And so I think we have got a really long way to go.

You know, just a couple of the examples that were given—Honduras is one. I mean, there is no way that that can be considered a government that is trying to improve on corruption. Egypt is another. Egypt is a really big problem in the whole terrorism context.

The CHAIRMAN. Mr. Gershman, any additional thoughts in that regard?

Mr. GERSHMAN. Well, Senator, in my testimony I used the term the "objective alliance" to describe the relationship between the kleptocrats and the financial system. You saw evidence of this in the "60 Minutes" program about global witness where somebody impersonating a corrupt figure in Africa went to 14 New York law firms to get help in avoiding the law really, and 13 of the 14 law firms were prepared to help him. Only one said no. So there is a kind of hypocrisy there, especially if we are at the same time preaching and promoting democratic values.

So I think one thing that we could do is begin to address this objective alliance—Senator Menendez was getting at it when he focused attention on the issue I raised about the enablers. And there it is a matter of transparency. It is a matter of naming and shaming. It is a matter of figuring out ways in which through law we can prevent the receipt of these funds.

I mean, we support people in these countries, investigative journalists, civil society activists, and so forth, who are trying to prevent the theft of the money, but we have to do more to prevent its receipt in our financial system, which is preceded by a laundering process and then all the other things. I think if we can be more consistent in our behavior by breaking this link between the kleptocrats and our own system, I think that would do some good.

The CHAIRMAN. Well, let us follow up a little bit on that. I mean, we have U.S. national interests all over the world. It seems to me that some of the countries we deal with have cultures that are somewhat more like ours. Some of them are very different. And we have to deal with the world as it exists, not as we would wish for it to be. We hope to get it to a different place through our involvement and leadership.

But let us go back to Afghanistan, which I think is just a great example. I know Ms. Chayes has spent a lot of time there. Afghanistan is a country, whether we like it or not, whose culture is built, has been built on corruption for years at almost every level.

And when we were referring, by the way, to public officials, we were not referring to the current public official, leader of the country, there who I do think is, to the extent he can, genuinely trying to deal with the corruption issue.

But, for instance, in Afghanistan, just to use that, lots of U.S. dollars are flowing into there, lots of other countries' dollars are flowing in there. If you went to zero tolerance, as it relates to corruption, I think a fair analysis would say that the government would likely fail pretty quickly there. I am just being fair in my assessment. So how do we deal with that? So here we are dealing within a country that we know tremendous corruption takes place. I am sure we are being viewed by the citizens there as enabling corruption, but corruption is a way of life there, not that we are directly involved in corruption necessarily today, but let us face it in some ways have been for influence reasons.

How do we deal with that? The world is not exactly the way we would wish for it to be, and we have some pretty big national interests at stake.

Ms. CHAYES. I think it really has to do with shaping the broad range of our approaches. So it means you are not in a position where it is either a blank check or cut off—or zero tolerance. But you say, okay, we are now working in an environment where this is a very significant aspect of how things are done and a very significant aspect of our national interests because it is driving people into the arms of the enemy.

Therefore, in that case, if we are providing education funding, for example, the number of schools is no longer the only measure that we use. It is the number of schools and the lack of shakedowns by teachers against students. Right? That becomes equally important to the number of schools. And then you do the political economy analysis, figure out, do network analysis and figure out, wow, who are some of the really critical individuals who may be, for example, a nexus between the criminal world, the Taliban world, and the government. There are individuals that were triple-hatted in those networks. And you say these are the people who are priority for some of the types of sanctioning that you gentlemen were discussing earlier, for example, visa bans. It does not have to be throw the guy in jail. There is a whole variety—at least do not fly him around in our helicopters and begin, therefore, to use the programming and the interactions that we are having as a way of changing the incentive sub-structure operating on them.

The CHAIRMAN. Mr. Gershman?

Mr. GERSHMAN. Senator, when I was speaking earlier about China, I mentioned that the people who are fighting against corruption identify themselves with universal values, and this is millions upon millions of people in China. The regime would promote nationalism, saying we are different from the West. This reminds me of the debate in the 1990s over Asian values when Li Kuan Yew would promote that line saying democracy was not consistent with Asian values, which are more top down and do not emphasize the individual as much, and Kim Dae-jung came back with very powerful and articulate arguments rooting these universal values in Asian culture.

When we created the world movement for democracy in India, a non-Western country, in 1999, Amartya Sen came to the meeting and gave a talk where he talked about how the rootedness of Indian culture in values having to do with individual rights and the accountability of government officials.

So these are really universal values, and I think what is going on today in the world is a struggle between people who are affirming these values, which are not narrowly Western values but are universal values embodied in the universal declaration, and regimes that would like to use the argument of traditional culture as being inconsistent with these values to defend what they are doing.

And I do not think we should let them get away with it. I think we should affirm our values as universal values and then identify with and support the people in these countries and cultures that want to progress and try to adapt their system to the modern world which requires transparency and the rule of law if these countries are going to develop economically because it is in the interest of these countries to have the rule of law, to have transparency, to observe these so-called universal values. And I think we have allies there, and I do not think we should assume that because of cultural differences, somehow they are at the other side of the world and we do not have anything in common with them.

The CHAIRMAN. I think that is a great assessment.

I would add that there is another tension at work here, and that is the tension between expediency and going at it sort of the long, hard way. I think that sometimes we allow certain agencies within our government to operate, especially when we have concerns about U.S. lives at stake and military operations that may be underway. The expediency of enabling additional corruption versus doing the work in a much more difficult way, which by the way, could in fact, in fairness, cause additional U.S. lives to be at greater risk in the short term, which is obviously something that we do not want to see happen. So I think we have numbers of tensions that exist around this issue.

You look like you want to say something.

Senator CARDIN. I just really wanted to thank the witnesses. The chairman can read me very well. I just really want to thank the witnesses and thank the chairman, if I might, for this hearing. It has been typical of Senator Corker's leadership in this committee, if I can just take one moment. This hearing is particularly important as we deal with corruption and how we can come together with greater administration action and perhaps legislative action to help.

This committee has taken on many tough issues in this Congress. We have taken on oversight of important foreign policy decisions. We have spoken out in many regions and in many countries with resolutions from this committee that clearly go on the record as to our concerns. We have been able to give additional tools to the administration to deal with human rights violations, to deal with corruption, and to deal with nuclear proliferation. And we have done that without ever having a partisan division in this committee. I do not think any other committee in the Congress has the type of record that we have in avoiding the pitfall of an election year politics.

And I agree with the chairman's assessment. We are going to take a look at the corruption issue. We are going to take a look at whether we can get additional tools done. We are going to do it in a bipartisan manner, and we are going to do it outside of the politics of this particular year. I just really wanted to thank the chairman for calling this hearing and for his leadership on these issues during the course of this Congress.

The CHAIRMAN. Well, thank you, and I appreciate you and your staff pressing for these types of hearings and this hearing in particular. And thank our outstanding witnesses not only for being here today but the advice and knowledge and wisdom that you share with us in our offices from time to time.

If you would, we will have some written questions. I know a number of members left because our voting schedule ended last night. If you could respond fairly promptly, as you will, I know. The record will be open until the close of business on Monday. We thank you both for your leadership on this issue and so many others.

And with that, the committee is adjourned.

[Whereupon, at 12:24 p.m., the hearing was adjourned.]

ADDITIONAL MATERIAL SUBMITTED FOR THE RECORD

STATEMENT SUBMITTED BY THE U.S. DEPARTMENT OF JUSTICE

INTRODUCTION

The Department of Justice (the Department, DOJ) appreciates the opportunity to submit this Statement for the Record as Congress considers the important and complex topic of combatting international corruption. The Department has a strong commitment to, and record of, fighting overseas corruption, both through our own law enforcement actions, and through building the capacity of our foreign law enforcement partners to take actions to fight corruption themselves.

As explained below, however, DOJ does not currently receive direct funding from Congress for our overseas capacity-building programs, and receives only a fraction of the funding necessary to cover the headquarters costs of administering those programs. Instead, DOJ must apply to the State Department or other U.S. government funders to receive foreign assistance funds for its capacity-building programs, and must cover the majority of its headquarters costs by charging overhead in its Interagency Agreements with the State Department. The Senate Commerce, Justice, Science, and Related Agencies (CJS) Appropriations Subcommittee has noted that it is "concerned" about "the instability of budget and staffing challenges" faced by DOJ's overseas capacity-building programs under the current funding model. The Administration is committed to seeking a solution to this problem, to ensure that DOJ can continue to help other countries fight international corruption, to the benefit of their citizens and our own.

DOJ'S ANTI-CORRUPTION LEGISLATIVE PROPOSALS

In May 2016, DOJ put forth legislative proposals that, if enacted, would strengthen our anti-corruption authorities and close the gaps in U.S. law that are open to abuse by bad actors. Specifically, DOJ proposed legislation that would increase transparency into the beneficial ownership of companies formed in the United States and would provide additional law enforcement tools to combat corruption and money laundering. The legislation would enhance law enforcement's ability to prevent bad actors from concealing and laundering illegal proceeds of transnational corruption and would require reporting of beneficial ownership of corporations, which would aid law enforcement in the prevention and investigation of financial crimes.

DOJ'S ANTI-CORRUPTION PROGRAMS

DOJ's commitment to investigating and prosecuting international corruption is reflected in a number of different programs, including:

- *Foreign Corrupt Practices Act (FCPA) Unit:* DOJ's FCPA Unit consists of a select group of approximately 30 prosecutors. The unit works with the Federal Bureau of Investigation's (FBI) International Corruption Unit and its three dedicated International Corruption Squads, as well as other investigative agencies, to investigate and prosecute individuals and corporations that pay bribes to foreign officials in order to obtain or retain business. The FCPA Unit routinely works with its foreign law enforcement partners in corruption cases, in countries such as Belgium, Brazil, Colombia, Cyprus, France, Germany, Indonesia, Ireland, Italy, Latvia, Luxembourg, the Netherlands, Norway, Panama, the Philippines, Saudi Arabia, Singapore, Sweden, Switzerland, Taiwan, and the United Kingdom, among others. Recent case resolutions include *United States* v. *Alstom S.A. et al.* ($772,290,000 criminal penalty), *United States* v. *VimpelCom* ($230 million criminal penalty and a global penalty and disgorgement of $795 million with the Securities and Exchange Commission (SEC) and Dutch Prosecution Service), and *United States* v. *Roberto Rincon et al.* (guilty pleas of six individuals who paid and received bribes).

- *Kleptocracy Initiative:* DOJ's Kleptocracy Unit consists of approximately 16 experienced and highly-trained prosecutors who work with agents from the FBI, the Internal Revenue Service (IRS), and the Department of Homeland Security (DHS), and with U.S. Attorney's Offices around the country. The Unit investigates and prosecutes acts of high-level foreign corruption—such as bribery, embezzlement, and money laundering—that affect the U.S. financial system. The Unit also brings asset recovery actions to forfeit the proceeds of foreign official corruption in which, as appropriate, the proceeds are returned for the benefit of the citizens of the foreign countries that were victimized by that corruption. Recent successful cases include those leading to the recovery of approximately $30 million in bribe proceeds paid to a former President of the Republic of Korea, $30 million in embezzled and extorted funds obtained by the Second Vice President of Equatorial Guinea, and approximately $115 million in corruption proceeds derived from illicit payments to senior officials of the Government of Kazakhstan. Through these and other asset recovery actions, the Kleptocracy Initiative has restrained more than $1.8 billion worldwide, and will soon have returned more than $150 million to victims of foreign corruption.

- Prosecution of Fraud on U.S. International Assistance Programs: DOJ's Fraud and Public Integrity Sections investigate and prosecute individuals who embezzle, steal, or obtain by fraud or bribery U.S. federal program funds, including foreign assistance funds. Recent cases include: *United States* v. *Lee, et al.* (U.S. military officers, military contractors, and related co-conspirators convicted of participating in a scheme involving the payment of over $1.27 million in bribes in exchange for obtaining bottled water and other contracts at Camp Arifjan in Kuwait); *United States* v. *Kline* (U.S. soldier charged with soliciting gratuities from Afghan contractors doing business with the U.S. military); and *United States* v. *Green* (U.S. contractor charged with soliciting bribes from an Afghan firm seeking contracts with the U.S. Agency for International Development (USAID) relating to agricultural development).

DOJ'S INTERNATIONAL PARTNERSHIPS TO FIGHT CORRUPTION

DOJ cannot fight international corruption alone; it is essential that we have strong and competent foreign counterparts, both to cooperate in our investigations and prosecutions, and to investigate and prosecute their own corruption cases. To achieve this end, DOJ has pursued three strategies:

First, Build an International Consensus and Framework to Fight Corruption

DOJ has taken the lead in working with the State Department to develop multilateral organizations focused on fighting corruption, including the Organization for Economic Co-operation and Development (OECD) Working Group on Bribery; and, with the strong support of the Senate Foreign Relations Committee, DOJ worked with the State Department to create a key multilateral instrument—the UN Convention Against Corruption—which establishes that the fight against corruption is a universal goal, and which furthers that goal by setting out agreed-upon offenses that must be criminalized as well as preventive policies that should be followed.

Second, Build Effective Law Enforcement Cooperation Mechanisms

Again with the support of the Senate Foreign Relations Committee, DOJ and the State Department have negotiated and entered into many bilateral mutual legal assistance and extradition treaties that are essential to international investigations and prosecutions of corruption; DOJ has also vastly expanded the size of its Office of International Affairs and established the Central Authorities Initiative to help other countries improve their ability to cooperate in international investigations.

Third, Build the Capacity of Foreign Counterparts to Investigate and Prosecute Corruption

Corruption, left unchecked, can destabilize societies, leaving them—and, by extension, the United States—vulnerable to transnational organized crime and terrorism. Therefore, to protect both foreign citizens and our own, it is critical that in addition to bringing our prosecutions, we enhance the capability of foreign countries to fight corruption within their societies. One of the most effective ways of accomplishing this goal is through long-term capacity-building partnerships between foreign and DOJ prosecutors and law enforcement experts. DOJ has two offices dedicated to this task: the Office of Overseas Prosecutorial Development Assistance and Training (OPDAT) and the International Criminal Investigative Training Assistance Program (ICITAP). OPDAT and ICITAP are funded principally via interagency agreements with the State Department. By sending federal prosecutors and law enforcement experts to reside and work with their foreign counterparts for multi-year periods, OPDAT and ICITAP have achieved remarkable results—including the creation of dedicated foreign anti-corruption task forces—at very small cost to the United States. The work that OPDAT and ICITAP have done in this area has frequently resulted in increased credibility and public legitimacy of the foreign government's criminal justice systems.

For example:

- In Honduras, OPDAT Resident Legal Advisors recently worked with the local prosecution services on several significant anti-corruption cases, including the prosecution of a former judge for receiving bribes in exchange for acquitting a notorious drug dealer of murder charges, for which the judge was ultimately sentenced to five and a half years' imprisonment; and the seizure of millions of dollars in assets from a board member of the Honduran Institute for Social Insurance who stole over $350 million from the agency and who remains a fugitive;

- In Montenegro, ICITAP advisors have provided training and mentorship to the Organized Crime and Corruption Unit, as well as to the Financial Investigations Unit within the Criminal Police, including helping the Special Prosecutor seize over 20 million Euros in criminal assets that will be returned to the government of Montenegro;

- In Albania, OPDAT Resident Legal Advisors have provided case-based mentoring to the Albanian Serious Crimes Prosecution Office that has resulted in the arrests of two prosecutors and one police officer in unrelated corruption cases centered around the acceptance of bribes in exchange for providing favorable dispositions to criminals in pending court matters;

- In Indonesia, OPDAT Resident Legal Advisors have provided training and case-based mentoring to the Attorney General's Office and the Corruption Eradication Commission that resulted in the conviction of a provincial governor, ten mayors, and a number of other political figures for bribery. In addition, ICITAP advisors provided analytical training to the Financial Transaction Reports Analysis Center which enabled the Center to conduct over 100 corruption, asset forfeiture, and fraud-related financial investigations in recent years.

In 2016, Congress appropriated an increase of $1.5 million for OPDAT and ICITAP, bringing the current annual direct funding level to $4.1 million. The 2017 President's Budget includes a request for an additional $5 million in base resources for headquarters support. As presently structured, most of the funding spent annually on OPDAT and ICITAP headquarters and field operations (in excess of $100 million) comes from Interagency Agreements with the State Department. Most critically, there remains a requirement for appropriated base funding to stabilize headquarters operations. The Senate CJS Subcommittee restated again this year that it "remains concerned about the instability of budget and staffing challenges faced by [OPDAT] and [ICITAP] under the current funding structure provided via the Department of State." We appreciate Congress's support as the Administration continues to implement and refine whole-of-government security sector assistance programs and we continue to seek more direct headquarters support funding for OPDAT and ICITAP so that they can continue this critical anti-corruption work.

CONCLUSION

The Department of Justice remains committed to fighting corruption domestically and internationally through law enforcement action and by providing capacity-building assistance to foreign governments. The Department looks forward to working with the Congress to identify additional funding to improve its anti-corruption programs and thanks the Committee for its interest in these critical issues.

RESPONSES OF GAYLE SMITH TO QUESTIONS FOR THE
RECORD SUBMITTED BY SENATOR RUBIO

Question 1. USAID has indicated that congressional restrictions on providing police assistance, particularly section 660 of the Foreign Assistance Act of 1961, limit its ability to align its anti-corruption prevention and education programming with enforcement efforts.

♦ Has USAID updated its anti-corruption strategy since 2005?

♦ To what extent does section 660 still present an obstacle to whole-of-government anti-corruption programming?

Answer. Rather than update the 2005 anti-corruption strategy, USAID has incorporated its strategic approach to anti-corruption efforts within the broader strategy for Democracy, Human Rights and Governance (DRG), which was approved in 2013. The Agency's DRG Strategy focuses DRG programming around efforts proven to build more transparent and accountable government institutions. The DRG strategy emphasizes the need to integrate good governance elements into Agency efforts to alleviate extreme poverty, promote food security, improve health, education, and advance other development goals. It focuses efforts primarily on preventive measures, including efforts to boost transparency and effectiveness of public sector functions that are vulnerable to corruption, including procurement, public spending and investment, and public service delivery.

The new strategic approach also includes innovations such as Political-Economy Analysis (PEA) and other tools that ensure USAID is using a broad, critical lens to address corruption. Applied PEA is a field-research methodology used to explore not simply what and how things happen in development programming, but why things happen. It results in specific programmatic recommendations for a Country Development Cooperation Strategy (CDCS), project or activity design, including suggestions for course correction during implementation, or an evaluation. For example, USAID missions have used the Applied PEA approach to delve deeper into the incentives and power dynamics in sectors such as health and economic growth. The results have been used to design new activities or adjust programming to better fit the local context. These multilateral initiatives help support USAID's own anticorruption efforts by leveraging funding from, and coordinating activities with, other bilateral and multilateral donors and international organizations working to combat corruption and promote global standards for transparency and accountability.

In addition, USAID works at the multilateral level on anticorruption efforts to promote global standards for transparency and accountability, including the Extractive Industries Transparency Initiative, the Open Government Partnership, and the Effective Institutions Platform.

As a result of several changes in law, USAID can carry out a range of anti-corruption programming with or through police and other law enforcement forces notwithstanding Section 660 of the Foreign Assistance Act or under specific statutory exceptions to that restriction. As such, Section 660 presents little obstacle to USAID anticorruption programming. USAID has embraced these changes and actively engages law enforcement actors and institutions, as well as tax and customs agencies in anti-corruption efforts. In Central America and the Caribbean, for example, USAID programs include support for community-based policing programs.

In addition, Agency policies, including the "Assistance for Civilian Policing" policy, and practice guides, such as "The Field Guide for USAID Democracy and Governance Officers: Assistance to Civilian Law Enforcement in Developing Countries," include guidance on how to address corruption when providing assistance to law enforcement.

Question 2. With how critical each U.S. dollar spent abroad is, what systems are currently in place to ensure our foreign aid is not itself stolen by corrupt officials?

Answer. USAID is committed to accountability, transparency and oversight of U.S. government funds and has a number of mechanisms for ensuring funds are not lost to waste, fraud or abuse. The Agency relies upon its financial systems and controls as well as internal and independent audits to effectively manage, track and safeguard funds.

Prior to awarding funds, USAID Contracting/Agreements Officers make a pre-award responsibility determination to confirm financial and programmatic capacity to receive U.S. Government funding. They also ensure that regulatory language from the Federal Acquisition Regulation and Agency policy is included in each award. This regulatory language enables oversight and performance monitoring.

During the implementation of an award, USAID personnel closely monitor the contractor's or grantee's performance through a review of quarterly reports, site visits, and other means to oversee program performance. USAID personnel are trained to scrutinize all invoices submitted by awardees prior to approval. If there appear to be inconsistencies in the vouchers or concerns related to billed costs, these issues are elevated for additional review. External program and project evaluations of awards at various phases of implementation constitute additional oversight tools with respect to program costs and performance.

In the case of grant funds disbursed directly to host or partner governments, USAID utilizes the Public Financial Management Risk Assessment Framework (PFMRAF), a risk management process to identify, mitigate and manage the fiduciary risks encountered when considering direct assistance to foreign governments. It focuses on fiduciary risks to which USG funds may be exposed when administered directly by the public financial management systems of a country. This includes review of national-level entities, such as the Ministry of Finance, as well as sector-specific entities with whom we implement development activities, such as the Ministry of Health. The PFMRAF is a rigorous process designed to make sure that foreign assistance is not lost to waste, fraud, or abuse—assessing not only the public financial management environment of the partner country government, but also governance and public accountability factors, including legal and regulatory matters, as well as political will for non-corrupt, transparent, accountable, and effective governance.

In addition, USAID's Office of Inspector General (OIG) provides independent oversight of development programs around the world. The OIG carries out audit and investigative activities in about 100 countries, executing on this mission from offices in 12 locations, from Haiti to the Philippines.

Question. In the Western Hemisphere we've had several instances of private U.S. charitable contributions being wasted or exploited by local officials. Does USAID or any other element of the U.S. government work with private charitable entities to help them ensure that their activities in other countries are not wasted or counterproductive?

Answer. USAID supports a number of efforts in Latin America and the Caribbean that help ensure donor contributions are not wasted or misused. For example, USAID missions in this region regularly participate in donor roundtables to discuss the effective use of resources, including how to avoid duplication of efforts or mismanagement of funds. In Honduras, the USAID mission co-hosts an annual meeting that includes the participation of charitable groups to better coordinate the effective use of donor resources and promote long term sustainable assistance strategies.

In addition, USAID supports the Private Voluntary Organization (PVO) Registry, an online database of tax-exempt, nonprofits that have been vetted against the eight conditions of registration set out in 22 CFR 203. This database is open to the public and provides an overview of each registered organization's mission, expertise, geographic presence, activities, budget, and contact information. Each year, data provided by these PVOs are compiled and released as the Report of Voluntary Agencies Engaged in Overseas Relief and Development. All organizations meeting the definition of a PVO and looking to compete for grant funding from USAID are encouraged to register. This helps to streamline the review and approval of funding for some of USAID's NGO partners.

In addition, the Agency's investments in improving transparency and accountability and reducing fraud and corruption can help enhance the impact of official development assistance and private U.S. charitable contributions alike.

USAID exercises due diligence prior to awarding funds or partnering with private, charitable organizations anywhere in the world, including Latin America and the Caribbean. This includes ensuring that organizations that receive USAID funds have proper systems in place to manage and account for funds and any funds sub-granted or sub-contracted to other organizations or companies. Once funds are awarded, USAID closely monitors the use of those funds. External evaluations may be conducted on awards at various phases of implementation. Should allegations about the waste or misuse of our assistance arise, then USAID's Office of the Inspector General will launch an investigation. Investigations that lead to findings of fraud, waste or abuse of USAID resources can result in the termination of awards and criminal prosecution.

RESPONSES OF TOM MALINOWSKI TO QUESTIONS FOR THE
RECORD SUBMITTED BY SENATOR RUBIO

Question. Why haven't individuals like Cabello, El-Aissami, Merino, and the FARC been sanctioned? How much longer do we have to wait to stop this abuse of our financial system?

Answer. The steps we have taken to restrict visa eligibility and the sanctions we have imposed thus far through Executive Order 13692 have sent a clear message that the United States does not welcome money or travel of those who are responsible for or complicit in serious human rights violations and abuses, undermining democratic processes or institutions, or public corruption in Venezuela.

In addition, the United States has designated the FARC and the National Liberation Army of Colombia (ELN) for their terrorist and other illicit activities under a variety of other authorities. For example, the Secretary of State has designated both organizations as Foreign Terrorist Organizations (FTO) pursuant to section 219 of the Immigration and Nationality Act (INA) and as Specially Designated Global Terrorist entities under Executive Order 13224. In addition, the FARC has been designated under the Foreign Narcotics Kingpin Act. The consequences of these designations include a general prohibition against knowingly providing, or attempting or conspiring to provide, material support or resources to, or engaging in transactions with, these groups and the freezing of all property and interests in property of these organizations that are in the United States, or come within the United States or the control of U.S. persons. Moreover, as a consequence of the FTO designation, individuals associated with these organizations may be ineligible for a visa or are otherwise inadmissible to the United States.

We will continue to monitor these issues closely and stand prepared to take action against others as additional information that meets the criteria for sanctions becomes available.

Question. Does the USG have a coordinated campaign and inter-agency strategy for dealing with corruption and kleptocracy in foreign nations?

Answer. Yes, the interagency works together to combat corruption and kleptocracy to advance a set of policy goals and apply a range of tools that complement and reinforce each other. These efforts are best summarized as a three-pronged approach that we are working consistently to strengthen: to build greater transparency globally, to support the exposure of corruption at the highest levels through support for civil society led investigations and advocacy, and to ensure strong law enforcement. This is in addition to support provided by the Department of State and USAID to build the capacity of reformers and strengthen institutions through our democracy and governance work in countries where there's strong political will.

Since adopting the Foreign Corrupt Practices Act (FCPA), the United States has been a global leader in anti-corruption and, under this Administration, U.S. government agencies have developed a comprehensive, whole-of-government approach to enforce it. The Department of State leads on efforts to implement the UN Convention against Corruption (UNCAC) and other multilateral efforts to strengthen international transparency standards and practice, to broaden implementation of anti-bribery laws, and to promote responsible business conduct, while the Department of Commerce promotes transparency and anti-corruption efforts in our trading partners to create a level playing field for U.S. businesses. The Department of Treasury continues to press for strengthened beneficial ownership standards for all companies formed in the United States.

The Department of State and USAID are also ramping up our support for civil society led investigations that can uncover corruption across borders, inform local advocacy, and drive action by law enforcement through the development of a Global Anti-corruption Consortium. The Department of Justice (DOJ) launched the Kleptocracy Asset Recovery Initiative to pursue corrupt foreign officials who plunder state coffers for personal gain and then try to place those funds within the U.S. financial system, while the Department of Treasury enforces sanctions against persons who engage in official corruption and take advantage of the U.S. financial system. Meanwhile, the Millennium Challenge Corporation (MCC) and the Overseas Private Investment Corporation (OPIC) incentivize countries to demonstrate a positive track record and concrete plan to reduce corruption in order to achieve eligibility.

For the Department of State and USAID, global anti-corruption efforts also entail the promotion of human rights, participatory democracy, accountable and transparent governance, and economic empowerment more broadly. As Secretary Kerry has stated, fighting corruption must be treated as a first order national security priority, and the Administration is committed to strengthening and building on this range of efforts for the strongest possible impact.

Question. Does your bureau have an effective voice in these interagency efforts to combat these problems?

Answer. The Bureau of Democracy, Human Rights, and Labor's (DRL) Senior Advisor represents the bureau both within the Department and in the interagency to ensure it has an effective voice in efforts to combat corruption. Senior Department of State leadership is also strongly engaged in these efforts, including Secretary Kerry, who champions these efforts at the Cabinet-level and represented the U.S. government at the Global Anti-Corruption Summit hosted by the United Kingdom in May.

In addition, DRL leads U.S. government efforts on the Open Government Partnership and regularly monitors and reports on corruption issues globally in the annual Human Rights Report. Over the last several years, DRL's Global Programs office has increasingly prioritized support for civil society efforts to investigate and combat corruption around the world including recent efforts to build a Global Anti-corruption Consortium to support and scale this kind of work.

Question. How has the U.S. Government cooperated with foreign or international agencies to track down and punish corrupt leaders? What else can we do to enhance that inter-agency cooperation?

Answer. The Department of State leads much of the interagency coordination on multilateral efforts to both prevent and combat corruption globally. Our work with the G-20 Anticorruption Working Group helps us to collectively lead by example, to strengthen international anticorruption standards, coordinate donor support to developing countries, and strengthen standards within the G-20. The G-20 Denial of Entry Experts Network provides an opportunity for immigration and visa authorities to share best practices to deny safe haven to corrupt actors, while we work closely with our partners in the G-7 to coordinate a range of anti-corruption efforts, particularly since the Japanese presidency of the G-7 made anticorruption a priority.

While the Department of Justice would need to advise on U.S. civil or criminal actions against corrupt leaders, DRL works closely with the Departments of Justice and Treasury to develop strong corruption-related visa denial cases that reinforce the efforts of other agencies. Additionally, partners in civil society organizations often expose instances of corruption that can lead to investigations by law enforcement.

Question. Can you talk about the link between corruption and repressive regimes? Is it correct to say that corrupt regimes are more likely to deprive their citizens of their fundamental rights? How do our democracy and governance programs tackle this issue?

Answer. The Department of State often sees that repressive regimes cannot retain power without corruption and that corrupt regimes cannot remain in power without repression. At the same time, corruption presents a repressive regime's greatest vulnerability—it can often be a decisive factor in popular anger against the regime and ultimately contribute to its downfall. Meanwhile, when law enforcement and other government officials can be bought and sold, legal controls and protections for all citizens are at risk and insecurity is heightened.

The Department of State and USAID democracy and governance programs target the nexus between repression and corruption in a few ways. We work not only to build government capacity but also strengthen accountability by supporting civil society groups in exercising oversight over budgets, demanding transparency, and joining in participatory budgeting exercises. We support civil society-led investigations that expose corruption and generate demands for political change and action by law enforcement. We also support reformers in countries demonstrating the political will to tackle corruption. A good example of this is the work we do with our interagency partners in supporting justice system reforms in many different countries. This includes training and professional development opportunities for judges and prosecutors, empowering them to take on corrupt officials and elites.

Multilateral efforts offer an additional vehicle to elevate anti-corruption and empower local reformers. Seventy countries now participate in the Open Government Partnership (OGP), which helps governments and citizens harness new tools and technologies to fight corruption.

Question. Why hasn't the FARC or ELN been sanctioned?

Answer. The United States has designated the FARC and the National Liberation Army of Colombia (ELN) for their terrorist and other illicit activities under a variety of authorities. For example, the Secretary of State has designated both organizations as Foreign Terrorist Organizations (FTO) pursuant to Section 219 of the Immigration and Nationality Act (INA) and as Specially Designated Global Terrorist entities under Executive Order 13224. In addition, the FARC has been designated under the Foreign Narcotics Kingpin Act. The consequences of these designations include a general prohibition against knowingly providing, or attempting or conspiring to provide, material support or resources to, or engaging in transactions with, these groups and the freezing of all property and interests in property of these organizations that are in the United States, or come within the United States or the control of U.S. persons. Moreover, as a consequence of the FTO designation, individuals associated with these organizations may be ineligible for a visa or are otherwise inadmissible to the United States.

Question. How about other leaders of cartels or transnational organized criminal elements?

Answer. U.S. law and policy imposes significant restrictions on such individuals in terms of travel, use of the financial system, and criminal and civil penalties.

RESPONSES OF SARAH CHAYES TO QUESTIONS FOR THE
RECORD SUBMITTED BY SENATOR RUBIO

Question. What more can the U.S. Government be doing to help key regional actors tackle their institutional corruption issues?

Answer. By "regional," I assume Senator Rubio is referring to the Americas, but my answer holds—if in a somewhat attenuated fashion—elsewhere. The United States is the most important external influence on most Latin American countries, and is therefore likely to have more leverage there than in many other regions.

A distinction should be made between severely corrupt countries that can be considered to have undergone at least some degree of an anticorruption transition, or to be led by genuine reformers, and those that are unrepentant kleptocracies. In this hemisphere, Brazil and Guatemala are the most obvious examples of transitioning countries; further afield, the category includes Nigeria, Tunisia, and Ukraine.

In these transitioning cases, the United States disposes of at least some partners in the fight against corruption—but should beware of the temptation to over—reward a government that may have only partially transformed, thereby reinforcing residual or resilient corruption networks. In Brazil and Guatemala, for example, anticorruption partners reside primarily in the justice sector, and cannot single-handedly effect the kind of institutional changes required to prevent a new cast of corrupt actors from stepping into the void left by the removal of heads of state—as clearly seems to be happening in Brazil.

In these cases, collaboration and capacity-building within the justice sector have already proven their worth. Strategic targeting of U.S. Department of Justice kleptocracy initiative cases at officials connected to those who have resigned could reinforce the message sent by local judiciaries, and identify assets to seize and return—provided care is taken to ensure the funds are invested to the benefit of the people and their desired reforms, and do not fall into the hands of officials who are just as corrupt as the former leadership.

Special attention should be devoted to banks and real estate agents in Florida, Texas, and California. Their weak customer scrutiny has allowed an influx of suspect money and helped inflate bubbles, thus damaging the U.S. economy as well as facilitating and profiting from corruption.

The most significant assistance the United States could provide in Brazil and Guatemala would be to civil society activists and other reformers, to help them think through a comprehensive program of legal and institutional changes that could help profoundly alter the political culture, deterring corruption upstream of its perpetration. Such an agenda would be sweeping and ambitious, and should be focused on the establishment of meaningful independence for different branches and agencies of government, meaningful oversight of government functions, and empowered citizen engagement in that oversight process. It should not presume virtue on the part of the business community, since too often, kleptocratic networks are integrated across public and private (and criminal) sectors.

The whole gamut of U.S. engagement with these countries, including diplomatic interactions and assistance, military as well as civilian, should be reviewed with an eye toward how it can reinforce an incentive structure that selects for public integrity and discourages corruption.

First, it should be carefully conditioned upon progress on and adherence to the program above.

Second, in these cases and elsewhere, it is no longer acceptable for the use of a lever as strategic as military assistance to be left at the discretion of low-level program officers at the U.S. State Department Bureau of Political-Military Affairs or one of innumerable offices at the U.S. Department of Defense, who roll their eyes at the word corruption. Such young officials rarely bother to find out whether the unit their programs are supporting is the enforcement arm for a kleptocratic network, or is being deliberately pillaged of salaries and the equipment the United States provides.

The results in Iraq and Afghanistan have been instructive in recent years: both countries' militaries have dramatically under-performed given the resources and support they enjoyed; budgets have been looted; billions of dollars of U.S. equipment has fallen into enemy hands; and security has worsened, as has the level of government corruption. This is hardly evidence for how to use U.S. resources effectively to further national security objectives—much less anticorruption objectives.

Military assistance should no longer be treated as a party favor; clear objectives should be set, and should include governance objectives, and packages should be measured for effectiveness against those goals. Program officers must be well-versed in these strategic objectives. As part of this reform, anticorruption must be built into program goals and design and selection of partner units and individuals, for all U.S. military assistance provided to these countries.

The same applies to civilian assistance. It's not quite enough to say that USAID support doesn't go to governments. What contractors or implementing partners are selected? Who are their beneficial owners? Which private-sector actors are funded by U.S. supported development banks? How much U.S. oversight exists for activities conducted with U.S. provided or backed loans? Does the bare existence of a U.S. assistance program serve an image-laundering function?

Third, diplomatic engagements related to corruption should not be limited to "lecturing," quickly countermanded by the character of other interactions. Host-country officials should feel the difference in the way they are treated if they are looting their public treasuries or not.

Even the U.S. Department of Commerce has a role to play, in carefully scrutinizing the sectors into which it recommends U.S. investment. Some U.S. businesses might be considered external members of Latin American corruption networks, given the degree of their interpenetration with private sector strands of those networks, or their reliance on a thoroughly corrupt supply chain.

Finally, the CIA must not be exempt from this framing.

In countries that remain unrepentant kleptocracies, such as Venezuela or Honduras, there are not many actors to help. The effort should emphasize the negative incentives discouraging corrupt behavior listed above, and avoid capacity-building programs that provide image-laundering for corrupt officials if they don't actually reinforce corrupt practices or provide revenue streams that are captured by the recipients.

For Brazil, Colombia, Guatemala, Guyana, Honduras, Mexico, Paraguay, and Venezuela, as for the other 54 countries on the list provided in my written testimony, Congress should require a political economy analysis, along the lines sketched out in my recent paper, as part of any assistance authorization above a certain size, together with strategies for mitigating the likelihood that assistance will reinforce existing corruption.

The approach recommended above would require an unprecedented degree of collaboration across the U.S. interagency, and is, I grant, ambitious. But the degree of siloing and internal contradiction that currently exists effectively deprives the United States of a coherent foreign policy.

A final note for reflection: with respect to any country in this region, it is important to recognize the historical role of U.S. policies and officials in actively corrupting their Latin American partners or clients, in establishing an incentive structure that rewarded officials who could be counted on to do the United States' bidding, even at the expense of their own citizens, and in placing these officials beyond the reach of local checks and balances. The populations of these countries have long memories. They will not be easily convinced of U.S. good faith. And corrupt officials will be able to credibly brandish the specter of U.S. support—even if they don't actually enjoy it—long into the future.

○